THE ULTIMATE
Slow Cooker
COOKBOOK

To my dad, my ultimate hero. Thank you for always being such an inspiration to me … I love you, Dad.

PENGUIN MICHAEL JOSEPH

UK | USA | Canada | Ireland | Australia
India | New Zealand | South Africa

Penguin Michael Joseph is part of the Penguin Random House group of companies whose addresses can be found at global.penguinrandomhouse.com

Penguin
Random House
UK

First published 2023
001

Set in Tellumo
Design by Georgie Hewitt
Food styling by Katy McClelland and Troy Willis
Colour reproduction by Altaimage Ltd
Printed and bound in Italy by Printer Trento S.r.L.

The authorized representative in the EEA is Penguin Random House Ireland, Morrison Chambers, 32 Nassau Street, Dublin D02 YH68

A CIP catalogue record for this book is available from the British Library

ISBN: 978–0–241–66446–9

www.greenpenguin.co.uk

THE ULTIMATE
Slow Cooker
COOKBOOK

Quick, healthy and energy-saving
recipes for every occasion

Clare Andrews

MICHAEL JOSEPH

Contents

Introduction 6

The Recipes 30

Introd

uction

Welcome

Wow, what a crazy 2023 . . . If you'd have told me a year ago, I never would have believed that I'd be sat here now finishing up writing my second book! Thank you all so much for being part of this wonderful journey I have found myself on.

This book is all about something that has been part of my life since I first started to cook for myself: the slow cooker! I've always had a passion for cooking and good food, and it all started with my slow cooker. I was gifted one when I first left home and immediately fell in love with how simple and easy to use it was, and how delicious the meals I was able to make were! It's something that lots of us have at the back of the kitchen cupboard waiting to be dusted off to make delicious stews and casseroles in the colder months, but I am here to show you how much more it has to offer. Vibrant year-round food that is healthy, economical and delicious. Tick, tick, tick!

The success of my first book, *The Ultimate Air Fryer Cookbook*, has showed me how much people are feeling the pinch and looking for cheaper, more convenient alternatives to cooking their meals in a traditional oven. While on the surface air fryers and slow cookers may seem like polar opposites – one fast, one slow – dig a little deeper and you'll soon see that these handy gadgets are kitchen siblings, both providing an economic and convenient way of preparing food that will save their users time and money in the kitchen – I can't live without either! Whether you've been using your slow cooker for a while, you're in the market for one or you have one that's been left at the back of your kitchen cupboard, this recipe book is for you.

Times are tough for us all in one way or another, and with the cost of living rising ever higher, managing our household budgets and our day-to-day living just seems to be getting more and more tricky. In times like these, we must do what we can to make our life a little easier, and I hope this book does just that, even if in a small way. Within these pages you'll find recipes that I have been cooking for years, family favourites old and new and recipes developed specially for this book, pushing the boundaries of what even I thought was possible in a slow cooker.

The Ultimate Slow Cooker is here to inspire you and add new, easy and exciting recipes to your weekly meal planning. With a lot of these recipes, I encourage you to make them your own. Want more chilli? Add away! Not keen on the flavour of cumin? Leave it out! That's what I love about cooking – it's all about you, your tastes, your flavours!

I hope you enjoy this book as much as I've enjoyed creating these recipes for you.

Clare

What Is a Slow Cooker?

Slow cookers are incredibly convenient and easy-to-use electric cookers that can help you to create delicious home-cooked meals while you're on the go. They are also a cheaper alternative to using an oven and easily transportable, so that you can cook anywhere that has a power socket! There are so many varieties on the market now, from the classic type that simply cooks your food low and slow whilst you go about your day, to more modern versions that have multiple functions that allow you to braise your food before slow cooking it or even to pressure-cook. If, like me, you've had yours for years then there's no need to buy a new one – the idea here is to save money after all!

On its most basic level, a slow cooker is a device that cooks food slowly at a low temperature, over a number of hours. Cooking in this manner is very energy efficient, with the average slow cooker costing around as much to run as a standard electric lightbulb. This style of cooking is also a massive time saver, meaning the home cook can simply place a few ingredients in their cooker at the beginning of the day and come back later to a delicious meal that is ready to serve.

Slow cooking works especially well for cheaper cuts of meat, where slow cooking breaks down the connective tissue and transforms something that would be tough and sinewy when cooked fast, to something succulent and tender.

As with all appliances, it is vital that you always read and follow your slow cooker manufacturer's instructions before using because models will differ. Sometimes they will tell you to preheat your slow cooker before you add your food. You will find that by preheating you do get a much more even cook, though I don't find it's always necessary – especially when I am in a hurry! But again, what works for one slow cooker may not for another.

Slow cookers come in all shapes and sizes, so make sure that you're buying the right size for your family's needs. If you live on your own or are in a couple, a small 1.5 litre slow cooker will be more than adequate, but if you are in a larger family, opt for a 3.5 litre or even an extra-large 6.5 litre model. The recipes in this book generally serve 4 people, so are perfect for a medium/standard slow cooker, though they can easily be scaled up or down as needed. Ideally, you want to leave a gap all the way around the outside of your slow cooker whilst it is in use to keep your appliance from overheating.

Slow cookers are quick and easy to clean, depending on what you cook in them of course! Always check your manufacturer's instructions first with this. With most models, you can pop the cooking pot into the dishwasher or give it a quick wash in some soapy water. Allow your slow cooker to fully cool before placing it into water and always rinse thoroughly. There are also products on the market that you can use with a slow cooker that reduce the amount it needs washing, which I discuss in more detail on page 22.

The Benefits of Slow Cooking

Slow cookers are cheaper to run

Slow cookers consume significantly less energy than a conventional oven, using around the same amount of electricity as a standard lightbulb. Electricity usage does vary by model and setting, but across the board slow cookers run at a much lower wattage than ovens, which means that cooking something for 8 hours on low in the slow cooker is much more cost-effective than cooking the same meal for an hour in the oven or on the hob. With the current energy prices and food inflation, these wonderful machines can really help keep your day-to-day costs down.

Slow cookers are time savers

I know it seems counterintuitive to say this, especially as the word 'slow' is in the name, but slow cookers are very time efficient. The magic of the slow cooker is that whilst they are simmering away cooking up your delicious, healthy meal, you can be getting on with your day. A few minutes prep in the morning means that dinner can be on the table with minimal fuss at the end of a long, hard day. Preparing can also be done the day before, so all you need to do is remove your ingredients from the fridge and place into your slow cooker, pre-set the timer or just press start and away you go. Do bear in mind that the recipes in this book can be changed to fit into your lifestyle and I have included timings for cooking meals on both low and high settings where possible.

Slow cookers are healthier

As with the air fryer, you don't need oil when you use a slow cooker. You are also in charge of the amount of vegetables, meat and pulses that go in, so you have more control of the goodness on your plate. There are a lot of pre-made sauces on the market now and some are amazing alternatives to homemade. Whether you choose to use them or not, with a slow cooker you are in control of how much and how often you use them, you can adjust the amounts, add more vegetables, or take away as you see fit. Whether you are a parent trying to get your little one to their five a day, or wanting to increase your own vegetable intake, slow cookers are perfect for such scenarios.

Do Your Homework

Before you cook anything in your slow cooker, always make sure you read the manufacturer's instructions because each model will have its own requirements and settings. I've kept the recipe instructions general to give you a rough idea of how long each meal will take. You can finesse the recipe to the way your slow cooker cooks. I like to preheat my slow cooker before I use it to make sure the food cooks evenly but see what works for you. Getting to know your slow cooker won't take you long and when you do, you'll be making the most of the cost and time benefits it provides.

Cooking Charts

Use the charts on the next few pages as a guide for how long you need to cook certain staple ingredients in your slow cooker. These timings are estimates and slow cookers do differ, so make sure to always check that your food is cooked properly and to the correct temperature before consuming.

Beef

(If you have the time I would always recommend slow cooking beef on low, but if you need to cook quickly here are the high settings.)

INGREDIENT	WEIGHT/ QUANTITY	HIGH HOURS	LOW HOURS	INTERNAL TEMPERATURE
Brisket	1.5kg	4–5	7–8	91–95°C
Top side beef	1kg	4–5	6–7	55°C (rare) 65°C (medium) 75°C (well done)
Braising steak	1kg	3–4	6–7	52°C (rare) 63°C (medium) 71°C (well done)
Short ribs	1.4kg	4–5	7–8	91–95°C
Burgers	500g	2–3	3–4	71°C

Chicken

(Timings will vary depending on the size of your chicken pieces.)

INGREDIENT	WEIGHT/ QUANTITY	HIGH HOURS	LOW HOURS	INTERNAL TEMPERATURE
Whole chicken	1.5kg	3–4	5–6	75°C
Chicken breast (skinless, boneless)	2–3 pieces	3–4	5–6	75°C
Chicken legs/ thighs	4–6 pieces	3–4	5–6	75°C
Wings	1.4kg	2–3	3–4	75°C
Drumsticks	1.5kg	3–4	5–6	75°C

Pork

INGREDIENT	WEIGHT/ QUANTITY	HIGH HOURS	LOW HOURS	INTERNAL TEMPERATURE
Shoulder	1.5kg	3–4	7–8	63°C
Gammon joint	1.5kg	3–4	5–6 (roast after)	68°C
Pork loin	1.8kg	4–5	6–7	75°C
Sausages	400g	3–4	6–7	68°C
Pork chops	500g	3–4	6–7	75°C

Lamb

(If you have the time I would recommend cooking lamb shanks on low.)

INGREDIENT	WEIGHT/QUANTITY	HIGH HOURS	LOW HOURS	INTERNAL TEMPERATURE
Leg of lamb	1.2kg	3.5–4	6–7	62°C
Shoulder	1.8kg	4–5	7–8	90°C
Lamb shanks	4 pieces	3.5–4	6–7	62°C
Chops	400g	3–4	6–7	63°C

Potatoes

INGREDIENT	WEIGHT/QUANTITY	HIGH HOURS	LOW HOURS	NOTES
Jacket potatoes	4	5–6	7–8	Until fluffy
Sweet potatoes	4	5–6	7–8	Until soft
Roast potatoes	8	3–4	5–6	Until crispy
Wedges	750g	3–4	4–5	Until crispy

Vegetables & Grains

INGREDIENT	WEIGHT/QUANTITY	HIGH HOURS	LOW HOURS	NOTES
Corn on the cob	250g	3–4	5–6	Until tender
Cauliflower	400–450g	2–3	5–6	Until soft
Butternut squash	1kg	4–5	6–7	Until soft
Aubergine	300g	4–5	6–7	Until soft
Rice	2 mugs of rice to 4 mugs of water	1–1.5	2–2.5	Until fluffy

Which Slow Cooker Should I Buy?

You've made the decision to transform your kitchen to a more energy-efficient one, so now you just need to pick the right slow cooker to suit your lifestyle. There are a few things to consider when choosing the perfect one for you, so I hope my guide will give you some help in the right direction.

Slow cookers vary so much in size and shape, so always keep in mind your budget, size of your workspace and what inner dish/pot size will work best for you and the size of your family. They really can vary so much, so check the dimensions before purchasing.

Slow cookers start from around £50 and some models can cost over £200. The most expensive include lots of extras like pressure cooking and air frying settings that you may or may not need, so do your research to find what benefits you and your family. Remember, a slow cooker that is bigger and more expensive isn't always better, as if you are cooking for two people you don't need to go too big.

Check whether the model you are considering has a pre-set timer too; this way you can set your slow cooker to begin cooking during the day, so your meal is ready as you get home.

Some slow cookers are very precise with a digital setting, and others are just a dial with simple 1, 2, 3 or low, medium, high settings for easy cooking. They do all work differently, so please do bear that in mind when you're recreating my recipes.

It may also be worth checking if your slow cooker can go into the dishwasher. This can be a real game changer for your washing-up, so it may well help with your ultimate decision!

Slow Cooker Kit

Slow cookers are ready to use pretty much as soon as you unpack them. But, if like me you prefer things to be a little easier, I have listed here some options to make your slow cooking journey an even simpler one. You may find you have most of these things in your kitchen already!

Inserts

Silicon inserts or heatproof dishes are such great accessories to have. You can now purchase inserts that separate your food too, so two different dishes can cook alongside one another, saving you time. They also wash easily, so there is less mess and you won't need to wash your slow cooker insert pot as much. Just always make sure whatever you decide to buy fits into the slow cooker that you have.

Meat thermometer

A meat thermometer is invaluable for me. I mainly use mine for when I cook larger joints of meat. It can put your mind at rest, as you can make sure the meat is cooked throughout but not overcooked too. There are so many on the market, so do some research and check out which is best for you. You don't have to spend a lot to get a good one.

Sauces & cupboard staples

I sometimes use pre-made marinades and sauces. You can of course make your own, but it's good to know you can get some fantastic affordable sauces in the supermarket. These can save you time so you can get on with other tasks, and I'm all for time-saving. Just do what's right for you.

Slow cookers are ideal for cooking stews, curries and soups. In my cupboard, I always make sure I have tinned chopped tomatoes, coconut milk and a selection of tinned beans and pulses. Gravy granules and small pots of stocks as well as a variety of dried herbs and spices are also ideal to have to hand.

Freezer

I use fresh herbs in a few of the recipes, but I know you can't have fresh all the time. Have a go at growing them yourself in a pot on the windowsill, or a great little cheat is freezing them. I often freeze mine, especially if I only need a handful.

I use my freezer a lot, especially if I do a big batch cook, but remember to cool thoroughly before freezing. Thaw in the fridge before using and label all your food with what's in the container and the date you cooked the recipe. I find this saves time having to guess later!

Slow Cooker Basics

I reap the benefits of my slow cooker all year round, and although slow cookers are popularly associated with autumnal and wintry meals, they really are for spring and summer too. I wanted to include recipes suitable for the warmer months so that you can make the most of energy- and time-efficient cooking every day. It will be your best friend when cooking a summer BBQ or maybe your go-to appliance for when you have friends over for dinner. The Set & Forget section in this book is just perfect for such occasions.

Slow cookers are not just for your day-to-day stews and soups. I feel this wonderful appliance is underused and what I want to do within this recipe book is help you to maximize the potential of your slow cooker and be able to keep yours out all year round as a staple in your everyday cooking.

Preheating

Some of my recipes suggest to preheat your slow cooker. It's not always necessary to do this, but for some recipes I do suggest you do. Please do go with what you feel is best and what works well for your slow cooker. Lots of the newer slow cooker models have a pre-setting timer too, which hugely helps with your preheating and cooking times.

Tea towel method

In a few of my recipes I suggest placing a tea towel under the slow cooker lid. The tea towel will absorb the moisture and stop it from dripping onto your bake and making it soggy. If using this method, do not leave the slow cooker unattended. Always make sure you are nearby.

Cleaning

Most slow cooker pots will happily go into the dishwasher, but I suggest always checking the manufacturer's guidelines first. To help with cleaning, on page 22, I have some suggestions of accessories you can use to help maximize the potential of your slow cooker and minimize the washing-up.

About the Recipes

Each recipe in this book has been tried and tested in my own home. Some I've been cooking for many years for my friends and family. Other recipes I've adapted a little to feed a crowd and a few more have been passed down through the generations. The book is divided into six chapters, Breakfast & Brunch for tasty mornings, Set & Forget recipes that basically cook themselves, Everyday Classics are the core staples every home cook needs, Fakeaways for a weekend treat, Soups, Sides & Sauces for comfort and essentials, and delightful Desserts for effortless indulgence. The timings I have given are guidelines only, so do feel you can adjust them and always check your meat is cooked thoroughly before serving.

What I love about cooking the most, as I mentioned in my first book, is the ability to customize each dish to your tastes. We are all so different and what works for me may not work for you. So, do remember my recipes are a guideline and hopefully they will inspire you to add your own flair and flavours to each one. Do add, remove and mix it up as you see fit or to suit what's in your fridge. For example, my son doesn't like kidney beans, so I replace them by adding baked beans instead. Life's all about a balance and that's the message I try to get across. Embrace your differences and add the flavours that make you happy.

Feeding a crowd is one of my favourite things to do, but I also love a glass of wine and chatting to my guests. That's why slow cookers are perfect for entertaining. Let the slow cooker do the hard work for you and let it create delicious food that is packed with flavour, while you relax and mingle!

Slow cookers are relatively easy to use, so experiment with yours, get to know it and explore all the different settings and options to make sure you optimize your slow cooking experience. Whether you use your slow cooker every day, at the weekend, for entertaining or just occasionally, I hope this book can inspire you to create more dishes, to change your cooking routine and to embrace your slow cooker for its time-efficiency and ease, whatever the time of year.

The Ultimate Slow Cooker Cookbook

Rec

pes

Breakfast & Brunch

Berry Granola

COOK 3 hours on high **SERVES** 4–6

This is a perfect healthy breakfast. If you want it a little crispier, you could transfer the mixture to your air fryer and cook at 180°C for a final 5 minutes, stirring halfway, or cook in a preheated oven at 180°C/350°F/gas 4 for 10 minutes, stirring a few times throughout. The granola keeps well, so feel free to double the ingredients to make a larger batch, but do add a little more cooking time.

325g rolled oats
150g mixed seeds
75g flaked almonds
75g desiccated coconut
4 tbsp runny honey
4 tbsp coconut oil

To serve
Greek yoghurt
fresh fruit

1. Put all the ingredients into your slow cooker and give everything a good stir, making sure all the dry ingredients are coated with the coconut oil and honey. Leave the lid open a centimetre or two, to allow some of the steam to be released so you don't end up with soggy granola. Cook on high for 3 hours. Gently stir the mixture every so often to prevent it from burning.

2. Allow to cool before transferring to an airtight container. Serve with some Greek yoghurt and your favourite fruit.

Overnight Porridge

COOK 8 hours/overnight on low   **SERVES** 4–6

This recipe is so easy, as all you need to do is prepare it the night before, pop the slow cooker on and you will have breakfast ready in the morning! It's perfect for those busy mornings when you need to get the kids ready for school. You can change it up with the toppings; dried apricots and dates are favourites in our house.

150g rolled oats
1 tsp ground cinnamon
2 tbsp runny honey
1 x 400ml tin of coconut milk
400ml water

To serve
splash of milk (optional)
a small handful of flaked almonds
a handful of fresh berries
a drizzle of runny honey

1. Before you head to bed, put all your ingredients into your slow cooker and cook on low for 8 hours.

2. In the morning, add a splash of milk to make it smoother, if you'd like. Add your favourite toppings and serve.

Shakshuka

COOK 4 hours on low, then 20 minutes on high **SERVES** 4

When I was first introduced to shakshuka a few years back, I instantly fell in love with the flavours. I have since tried many variations of this classic dish but this is my favourite. For me, it's such a perfect way to start a weekend, along with a steaming-hot coffee and the morning paper. Sheer bliss.

2 x 400g tins of chopped
    tomatoes
2 onions, chopped
1 tsp chilli flakes
2 tsp ground cumin
1 tsp paprika
150ml vegetable stock
a handful of fresh spinach,
    chopped
8 eggs
sea salt and freshly ground black
    pepper

To serve
a handful of fresh parsley leaves,
    chopped
4–8 slices of bread, toasted

1. Pop the tomatoes, onion and dried spices into your slow cooker, pour in the stock and stir. Cook on low for 3 hours.

2. Add the spinach, season, stir, then cook for a further hour.

3. Make 8 indentations in the sauce with the back of a spoon and crack an egg into each indentation. Cook on high for around 20 minutes, or until the whites are set and the yolks still slightly runny (do keep an eye on them).

4. Divide the eggs and sauce among 4 plates. Serve sprinkled with fresh parsley and with some toast on the side.

Homemade Baked Beans

COOK 2 hours on high   **SERVES** 4

These beans are a real favourite at home. They're so versatile; if you have any left over, why not try serving them with sausage and mash too! Yum.

1 vegetable stock cube, crumbled
350ml boiling water
1 tsp garlic granules
1 tsp onion granules
1 tsp paprika
500g tomato passata
1 tbsp balsamic vinegar
3 x 400g tins of haricot beans
1 tsp chilli powder
sea salt and freshly ground black
   pepper

1. Mix the stock cube with the boiling water, then pour this into the slow cooker. Add the rest of the ingredients, stir thoroughly and season. Cook on high for 2 hours.

Healthy, Hearty Vegan Brekkie

COOK 2 hours on high   **SERVES** 2

This is a perfect weekend brekkie or brunch – and not just for vegans! Pop it on while you take the kids swimming or head out to take the dog for a walk, and it will be ready when you get back. A healthy and hearty dish to set you up for the day.

1 tbsp olive oil
1 large beef tomato, halved
1 large portobello mushroom
1 x 200g tin of baked beans
8 asparagus spears
sea salt and freshly ground black
   pepper

To serve
2 slices of rye bread, toasted

1. Drizzle a little oil over the tomato halves, then place them in your slow cooker. Depending on the size of your slow cooker, you can either place the mushroom in whole or slice it and arrange the slices around the tomato. Add the beans, then cook on high for 1 hour.

2. After an hour, add the asparagus and cook for another hour.

3. Season to taste and serve with toasted rye bread.

Set & Forget

Hearty Lamb Shanks

COOK 6 hours on low   **SERVES** 2

Lamb shanks are a timeless classic and perfect for any day of the week. The gravy is just divine; you will definitely need some bread to soak up all the loveliness! This works well if you want to double up the quantities, you will just need to increase the cooking time.

2 lamb shanks
2 sticks of celery, finely chopped
2 carrots, finely chopped
2 brown onions, finely chopped
2 cloves of garlic, crushed
1 x 400g tin of plum tomatoes
100ml lamb stock
2 tbsp balsamic vinegar
2 anchovy fillets
2 sprigs of fresh rosemary, leaves picked
1 tsp ground coriander
1 tsp chilli powder
sea salt and freshly ground black pepper

To serve

a handful of fresh parsley leaves, chopped (optional)
mashed potato
green beans
crusty bread

1. Heat a pan over a high heat, then sear the lamb for about 3–5 minutes until browned all over.

2. Put the celery, carrot, onion and garlic into your slow cooker along with the tinned tomatoes and stir. Add the stock, balsamic vinegar, anchovy fillets, rosemary leaves and the spices, then season well and stir again. Place your lamb on top and cook on low for 3 hours, then turn the shanks and cook for a further 3 hours.

3. Serve sprinkled with fresh parsley, alongside buttery mashed potato, green beans and crusty bread. Enjoy!

Moroccan Lamb

COOK 7 hours on low **SERVES** 4

This is perfect for a dinner party or maybe even a hearty Sunday Roast alternative.
I adore the aromas that flood around my kitchen as the dish slowly cooks. The
wonderful sweetness of the honey mixed with the spices is just heavenly.

750g diced lamb (neck or
    shoulder work well)
1 x 400g tin of chopped
    tomatoes
300ml chicken stock
1 large red onion, chopped
1 sweet potato, cut into chunks
2 carrots, chopped
1 tsp ground cumin
½ tsp ground turmeric
1 tsp paprika
1 tbsp harissa paste
thumb-sized piece of fresh ginger,
    peeled and grated
2 cloves of garlic, crushed
½ tsp chilli powder
1 tbsp runny honey
sea salt and freshly ground
    pepper
a handful of dried apricots,
    chopped

To serve
a handful of fresh coriander
    leaves
Yoghurt & Mint Raita (see
    page 160)
rice or couscous

1. Heat a pan over a high heat, then sear the lamb for around
5 minutes until browned on all sides. Transfer to your slow
cooker. Add the tinned tomatoes, stock, onion, sweet potato
and carrot and stir. Add the rest of the ingredients except the
apricots. Stir well and cook on low for 7 hours.

2. Add the chopped apricots and stir.

3. Serve scattered with fresh coriander, with raita and a side
of rice or couscous.

Beef & Mushroom Stroganoff

COOK 7 hours on low **SERVES** 4

A hearty and gorgeous dish. This is one of my all-time favourites and an absolute go-to when in need of comfort food.

100g porcini mushrooms
100ml boiling water
500g chuck or braising steak
1 large onion, finely sliced
300g button mushrooms, sliced
3 cloves of garlic, crushed
2 pickled gherkins, sliced
1 tbsp Worcestershire sauce
100ml beef stock
120g crème fraîche
sea salt and freshly ground black
    pepper

To serve

a handful of fresh parsley leaves,
    chopped
long grain rice
steamed broccoli

1. In a bowl, soak your porcini mushrooms in about 100ml boiling water and set aside.

2. Heat a frying pan over a high heat, then sear your beef for about 5 minutes until browned on all sides. Transfer to your slow cooker and add the onion, mushrooms, garlic, gherkins, Worcestershire sauce, paprika and beef stock.

3. Slice the porcini mushrooms and add to the slow cooker along with their soaking water (being careful not to add the grainy bits at the bottom). Season and stir well, then cook on low for 7 hours.

4. About 30 minutes before the end of the cooking time, stir in the crème fraîche.

5. Serve scattered with fresh parsley, alongside some long grain rice and buttered steamed broccoli.

Beef & Lentil Stew

COOK 6 hours on low   **SERVES** 4

The flavours in this dish blend so well together, I guarantee you will all be going in for seconds, if not thirds . . . You won't want it to end!

2 brown onions, finely chopped
2 tbsp ground cumin
2 tbsp soy sauce
1 carrot, grated
200ml beef stock
1 x 400g tin of chopped
    tomatoes
400g tomato passata
3 cloves of garlic, crushed
500g minced beef
1 tsp ground cinnamon
1 tsp ground turmeric
1 tsp ground ginger
1 tsp dried chilli
2 x 400g tins of brown lentils,
    drained and rinsed
sea salt and freshly ground black
    pepper

To serve
a handful of fresh mint leaves,
    chopped
brown rice

1. Put all the ingredients except the lentils into your slow cooker, season and stir. Cook on low for 6 hours.

2. One hour before the end of the cooking time, add the lentils and stir.

3. Serve scattered with chopped mint with a side of brown rice.

Sweet & Sticky Gammon Joint

COOK 4 hours on high or 7 hours on low   **SERVES** 6–8

This gammon is so succulent and utterly delicious. If you have some left over, why not add it to my Pea & Mint Soup (see page 152). Or, why not try serving it with a slice of grilled pineapple and some chunky chips. If you have some left over, treat yourself to a hearty ham and wholegrain mustard sandwich, on crusty white bread … heavenly.

3 oranges, zest removed and
    flesh sliced
1 bay leaf
15 cloves
575ml apple juice
1.2kg boneless gammon joint
2 tbsp wholegrain mustard
7 tbsp runny honey

1. Put the sliced oranges, bay leaf and cloves into the slow cooker and pour in the apple juice. Place the gammon joint in the slow cooker and cook on high for 4 hours or low for 7 hours.

2. Remove the gammon and allow to cool slightly.

3. To crisp up the skin, score it in a criss-cross pattern. Mix the mustard and honey in a small bowl, then brush this mixture over the ham and place in your air fryer for 15 minutes at 180°C or in the oven for 25 minutes at 190°C/375°F/gas 5 (if using the oven, keep basting it throughout).

Oxtail with a Guinness & Mustard Gravy

COOK 7–8 hours on low   **SERVES** 4

This is a perfect 'pop' recipe, where you just pop everything in and let the flavours do the talking! Also, it tastes even better the next day.

1 tsp plain flour
750g oxtail, cut into chunks
2 brown onions, chopped
2 large carrots, chopped
2 parsnips, chopped
2 tsp English mustard
250ml vegetable stock
575ml Guinness
sea salt and freshly ground black
    pepper

To serve
mashed potato
spring greens

1. Season the flour, then toss with the oxtail until it's fully coated.

2. Heat a pan over a high heat, then sear the oxtail for around 5 minutes until browned all over. Transfer to your slow cooker.

3. Add the onion, carrot and parsnip, then stir the mustard into the stock and pour this into the slow cooker along with the Guinness. Cook on low for 7–8 hours, stirring occasionally.

4. Serve with some buttery mashed potato and spring greens.

Ox Cheeks with Ale Gravy

COOK 8 hours on low   **SERVES** 4

Ox cheeks have such a fantastic depth of flavour and are relatively cheap to buy, too.
Slow cooking is the perfect method to get the most flavour out of them.

500g ox cheeks
1 tbsp olive oil
3 tsp garlic granules
1 tsp onion granules
1 Oxo cube, crumbled
2 large carrots, chopped
4 shallots, chopped
2 sticks of celery, chopped
575ml ale
300ml beef stock
2 tbsp Worcestershire sauce
1 tsp soy sauce
1 sprig of fresh rosemary
1 sprig of fresh thyme
1 bay leaf
sea salt and freshly ground black
    pepper

To serve
mashed potatoes
green beans

1. Start by brushing the ox cheeks with the olive oil. In a bowl, mix together the garlic granules, onion granules and crumbled Oxo cube, then rub this mixture over the cheeks.

2. Put the carrot, shallot and celery into your slow cooker; they will be the base for your gravy. Pop the cheeks on top and pour in your ale, beef stock, Worcestershire sauce and soy sauce. Add the sprigs of rosemary and thyme and the bay leaf, then season and cook on low for 8 hours.

3. When your cheeks have finished cooking, place onto a board and pull apart with 2 forks.

4. Pour the delicious gravy in the slow cooker through a sieve.

5. Serve with buttery mashed potato and steamed green beans.

Spaghetti Bolognese

COOK 4 hours on high or 8 hours on low   **SERVES** 4

I know it's been done thousands of times, but I just had to put this one in. It's one of my family's absolute favourites, a real crowd-pleaser and an ideal meal any time! It's a great one to pre-prepare, too, which is helpful if, like me, you're juggling a lot. Simply prepare it all the night before, leave it in the fridge (keep the stock out and add when you put the slow cooker on) and all you need to do in the morning is pop everything into your slow cooker and go about your business. For me, it's one of the best feelings knowing dinner will be ready when I get home. This recipe will give you some leftover bolognese for the next day – it's scrumptious as a topping for a jacket potato.

500g lean minced beef
300ml beef stock
1 x 400g tin of chopped
    tomatoes
5 closed cup mushrooms, finely
    chopped
1 stick of celery, sliced
1 onion, sliced
1 large carrot, finely chopped
1 tsp Bovril
1 tbsp brown sauce
2 tbsp red pesto
1 tbsp dried oregano
1 tsp paprika
2 tsp garlic paste
sea salt and freshly ground black
    pepper

To serve
150g spaghetti
a large handful of fresh basil
    leaves, torn
garlic bread
salad

1. Pop all the ingredients for the bolognese into your slow cooker, give it a good stir, season, then cook on high for 4 hours or low for 8. Time to sit back and relax … Feel free free to stir throughout, although it's not necessary (I do like a cheeky taste test halfway through cooking).

2. When the bolognese is ready, cook the spaghetti in a saucepan of salted boiling water according to the packet instructions.

3. Serve the spaghetti topped with the bolognese sauce and scattered with fresh basil, alongside garlic bread and a fresh, crisp salad.

Vegan Chilli Non Carne

COOK 6 hours on low   **SERVES** 4

This is a firm favourite in our house. Whether for family or friends, it's something I will always make and know everyone will love. Pop the slow cooker on at lunchtime and it will be ready for the evening – maximum flavour with minimum effort!

6 vegan sausages, sliced
2 brown onions, finely chopped
2 x 400g tins of chopped
    tomatoes
2 red peppers, deseeded and
    chopped
2 tsp ground cumin
1 large carrot, grated
1 stick of celery, finely chopped
½ tsp chilli powder
1 x 400g tin of mixed beans
2 cloves of garlic, grated
sea salt and freshly ground black
    pepper

To serve
rice
a handful of fresh coriander
    leaves
1 green chilli, finely chopped

1. Start by frying the sausages in a frying pan over a medium heat for 5 minutes, then transfer to your slow cooker. Add the rest of the ingredients, season, and stir everything together. Cook on low for 6 hours.

2. Serve with a side of rice and a sprinkle of chopped coriander and fresh green chilli.

Chilli Con Carne

COOK 6–7 hours on low   **SERVES** 4

I just had to put this recipe in here because it's my favourite way to cook chilli. My son isn't a fan of kidney beans, so if cooking for him, I replace them with a tin of baked beans. This is also a great recipe to batch-cook and freeze, or use any leftovers to top a baked potato for lunch the next day.

1 onion, finely chopped

1 pepper (any colour), deseeded and chopped

1 carrot, grated

2 cloves of garlic, crushed

300ml beef stock

500g minced beef

1 tbsp ground cumin

1 tsp ground turmeric

1 tsp chilli powder

1 tsp paprika

1 Oxo cube

1 tsp Marmite

1 tsp soy sauce

1 tbsp tomato purée

1 x 400g tin of red kidney beans, plus the liquid in the tin (or 1 x 400g tin of baked beans)

sea salt and freshly ground pepper

To serve

1 red chilli, finely chopped

a handful of fresh coriander leaves

rice

1. Start by putting the onion, pepper and carrot into your slow cooker, along with the garlic. Pour in the stock, add the mince, seasoning and spices, crumble in the Oxo cube and stir well. Add the Marmite, soy sauce, tomato purée and kidney beans. If you're using baked beans, I would add these an hour before the end of the cooking time, as they can go rather mushy. Cook on low for 6–7 hours.

2. Serve scattered with fresh chilli and coriander and a side of boiled rice.

Veggie Sausage & Pearl Barley Stew

COOK 6 hours on high   **SERVES** 4

We have at least two meat-free days a week at home and this recipe always goes down
so well as a tasty mid-week meal. I often have vegetarian sausages in the freezer and
pearl barley in the cupboard, which makes preparing this dish even easier.

2 carrots, finely chopped
1 large red onion, finely chopped
2 sticks of celery, finely chopped
1 litre vegetable stock
1 tsp dried oregano
1 tsp garlic granules
125g pearl barley
12 vegetarian sausages
sea salt and freshly ground black
    pepper

To serve
a handful of fresh parsley leaves

1. Put the carrot, onion, celery, stock, oregano, garlic granules
and pearl barley into your slow cooker.

2. Heat a pan over a medium heat, then add the sausages and
fry for around 5 minutes, just enough to brown the skin.
Alternatively, cook them in the air fryer at 180°C for 5 minutes
or in a 180°C/350°F/gas 4 oven for 10 minutes. Slice them in
half and add to the slow cooker. Cook on high for 6 hours.

3. After the cooking time, check the consistency before serving –
you may need to add a little boiling water to the sauce.

4. Sprinkle over the parsley and serve.

Stuffed Sweet Potatoes

COOK 6 hours on high   **SERVES** 4

This is an easy mid-week meal that everyone can enjoy! My family and I love how the mozzarella melts so deliciously into the sweet potato.

4 sweet potatoes
1 tbsp olive oil
250g pre-grated mozzarella
   cheese
10 slices of chorizo
8 sun-dried tomatoes, chopped
6 spring onions, thinly sliced
sea salt and freshly ground black
   pepper

1. Wash the sweet potatoes and prick gently with a fork. Drizzle with olive oil and season. Wrap each potato in a piece of tinfoil and seal tight. Place them in your slow cooker and cook on high for around 6 hours (depending on the size of your potatoes, you may need to adjust the time).

2. When cooked, slice open and top with the mozzarella, chorizo, sun-dried tomatoesand put under the grill or air fry at 180°C for a few minutes, until the cheese melts and the chorizo crisps up.

3. Sprinkle with the spring onions and enjoy.

Vegetable & Chickpea Summer Stew

COOK 7–8 hours on low   **SERVES** 4

This is such a great recipe to use vegetables that are in season, as they are cheaper and much fresher. This recipe is so easy and one you can prepare the day before; just pop the slow cooker on when you're ready. Less stress and your five a day in one dish – what's not to love! Make sure you chop all the vegetables into similar-sized pieces so they cook at the same rate.

3 courgettes, chopped
2 carrots, chopped
1 onion, chopped
1 aubergine, chopped
1 red pepper, deseeded and
    chopped
2 large baking potatoes, chopped
4 cloves of garlic, crushed
1 x 400g tin of chickpeas
1 x 400g tin of chopped
    tomatoes
2 tbsp olive oil
1 tsp red pesto
1 tsp dried parsley
1 tsp ground coriander
sea salt and freshly ground black
    pepper

To serve
a handful of fresh coriander
    leaves, chopped
4 tbsp red pesto
crusty bread

1. Put the courgette, carrot, onion, aubergine, red pepper, potato and garlic into your slow cooker. Pour in the chickpeas (with their liquid), along with the tinned tomatoes, olive oil and pesto. Add the parsley and coriander, season and stir. Cook on low for 7–8 hours, depending on the size of your potatoes.

2. Serve scattered with coriander, with a dollop of red pesto and some crusty bread on the side.

Pulled Pork Pittas

COOK 8 hours on low   **SERVES** 4

This is a great recipe to just let the slow cooker work its magic on the meat and the spices. Simply enjoy the meat falling apart after the cooking time.

1kg pork shoulder joint
2 cloves of garlic, crushed
3 tbsp white wine
150ml water
1 tsp chilli flakes
1 tsp garlic granules
2 tsp paprika
1 tbsp tomato ketchup
1 tbsp balsamic vinegar
2 tbsp brown sugar
sea salt and freshly ground black
    pepper

To serve
pitta breads
salad
Yoghurt & Mint Raita (see
    page 160)
4 handfuls of sweet potato fries,
    cooked from frozen
1 red chilli, chopped (optional)

1. Pat your pork dry with kitchen paper and place it in your slow cooker. Add the garlic and pour in the white wine.

2. In a jug or bowl, mix the water with the spices, ketchup, balsamic vinegar and sugar, then pour this over your pork. Season, then cook on low for 8 hours.

3. Serve in warmed pitta breads with salad and raita and a side of fries. If you prefer more of a spicy kick, add chopped fresh chillies, too!

The Ultimate Sloppy Joes

COOK 6 hours on low   **SERVES** 4

These should come with a warning, as they're not only super delicious, but super messy, too! I like to toast the buns a little before serving . . . Enjoy!

500g minced beef
1 onion, finely chopped
1 red pepper, deseeded and finely
    chopped
2 cloves of garlic, crushed
2 tsp paprika
5 tbsp tomato ketchup
1 tbsp brown sauce
300ml beef stock
1 tbsp Dijon mustard
1 tbsp balsamic vinegar
sea salt and freshly ground black
    pepper

To serve
4 brioche buns, toasted
4 slices of cheese (I use Monterey
    Jack)
sliced gherkins
spicy chilli sauce (optional)
2 large handfuls of oven chips,
    cooked from frozen

1. Add all the ingredients to your slow cooker, season and stir. Cook on low for 6 hours.

2. Spoon the filling onto the base of each brioche bun, top with the cheese, gherkins and a dash of spicy chilli sauce, if using, then finish with the other half of each bun.

3. Serve with a side of chips.

Sweet Potato, Butternut Squash & Spinach Curry

COOK 4–5 hours on low   **SERVES** 4

This is such a perfect mid-week recipe. All you need to do is pop your ingredients into the slow cooker and let the flavours do the hard work for you! Serve with basmati rice and tasty naan bread to soak up the incredible sauce.

2 sweet potatoes, peeled and cut into cubes
½ butternut squash, peeled, deseeded and cut into cubes
1 onion, sliced
2 cloves of garlic, grated
thumb-sized piece of fresh ginger, peeled and grated
1 tsp ground turmeric
1 tsp ground cumin
1 tsp garam masala
1 x 400ml tin of coconut milk
1 x 400g tin of chopped tomatoes
200ml vegetable stock
2 nuggets of frozen spinach or a handful of fresh spinach
sea salt and freshly ground black pepper

To serve
a handful of fresh coriander leaves
basmati rice
4 naan breads
mango chutney

1. Put the cubed sweet potato and butternut squash into your slow cooker. Add the onion, garlic, ginger, spices, coconut milk, tinned tomatoes and vegetable stock and stir well. Cook for 3–4 hours on low.

2. Add the spinach, stir, then cook for a further hour.

3. Season to taste and serve scattered with coriander, alongside basmati rice, warm naan breads and a dollop of mango chutney.

Everyday Classics

Cowgirl Stew

COOK 3–4 hours on low   **SERVES** 4

What I love about his recipe is it's so versatile. You also don't need to add the hot dogs; you can leave them out and just have this as a classic bean stew. I serve mine with a crusty baguette, but it's also great on a jacket potato. My son is not a fan of kidney beans, so when I'm cooking it for him, I simply leave them out and double up on the baked beans. This is what I love about cooking: mixing things up to suit different tastes. My recipes are just a guide. Go make it yours.

4 tinned or jarred hot dogs, cut into bite-sized pieces

1 onion, sliced

2 x 400g tins of chopped tomatoes

½ x 400g tin of red kidney beans, drained and rinsed

2 tbsp Worcestershire sauce

1 tbsp brown sauce

1 tsp cayenne pepper

1 tsp paprika

1 tbsp tomato purée

1 red pepper, deseeded and chopped (or a handful of frozen chopped peppers)

1 green pepper, deseeded and chopped (or a handful of frozen chopped peppers)

1 x 200g tin of baked beans

250ml vegetable stock

sea salt and freshly ground black pepper

To serve

crusty baguette or bread

1. Put the hot dogs into your slow cooker, along with the sliced onion. Follow with the chopped tomatoes, kidney beans, Worcestershire sauce, brown sauce, cayenne pepper, paprika and tomato purée. Stir and cook on low for 2 hours.

2. Add the peppers, vegetable stock and baked beans, season, then stir well. Cook for a further 1–2 hours. How long the peppers take to cook will depend on their size.

3. Enjoy by a warm, cosy fire with some crusty bread to dip into the rich, smoky sauce.

Lamb Stew

COOK 6 hours on low   **SERVES** 4

A great mid-week meal for the whole family to enjoy. Simple ingredients but packed with flavour. Once cooled, the stew can be frozen for up to 3 months.

1 tbsp plain flour
800g lamb shoulder, diced
3 carrots, chopped
1 large onion, chopped
650ml lamb stock
2 bay leaves
2 sprigs of fresh rosemary, leaves
    picked
sea salt and freshly ground black
    pepper

To serve
mashed potato
steamed spring greens

1. I like to preheat my slow cooker on low for 5 minutes but this is optional.

2. Season the flour, then toss with the diced lamb to coat. Heat a pan over a high heat, then sear the lamb for around 5 minutes until browned all over. Transfer to your slow cooker. Add the carrot, onion, lamb stock and herbs and stir. Cook on low for 6 hours.

3. Serve with buttery mash and greens.

Shepherd's Pie

COOK 7 hours on low   **SERVES** 4

**Hearty and delicious, this is a perfect winter warmer. When I make mashed potato,
I always make extra and freeze it for this recipe to make this meal even easier to prepare.**

500g lean minced lamb
125ml lamb stock
2 carrots, grated
1 stick of celery, finely chopped
1 onion, finely chopped
2 tbsp tomato ketchup
2 anchovy fillets
1 x 400g tin of chopped
    tomatoes
2 tbsp Worcestershire sauce
2 tsp chopped fresh rosemary
2 cloves of garlic, crushed
sea salt and freshly ground black
    pepper

For the topping
800g leftover mashed potato
a handful of grated Cheddar
    cheese
1 tsp dried parsley

To serve
onion gravy
steamed spring greens

1. Put all the ingredients into your slow cooker and stir well. Cook on low for 7 hours.

2. After 6 hours, warm up the mash either in the microwave for a few minutes or in a pan over a medium heat for about 5 minutes. Mix in the cheese and parsley, then spoon the topping over the filling in the slow cooker. Place a tea towel over the slow cooker, close the lid and cook for a further hour.

3. Serve with onion gravy, alongside some of your favourite greens.

Veggie Lancashire Hot Pot

COOK 5–6 hours on low **SERVES** 4

Even though this is meat free, it still has that delicious slow-cooked flavour we all know and love. The Worcestershire sauce just gives it that little added kick, but if you're vegetarian or vegan, Henderson's Relish is a perfect alternative. You will definitely want some crusty bread to soak up all the flavours on your plate, too; I guarantee you won't want to let any go to waste.

5–6 white potatoes, peeled
3 carrots, finely chopped
1 onion, finely chopped
500ml vegetable stock
3 cloves of garlic, crushed
150g chestnut mushrooms, sliced
60g tomato purée
2 tbsp Worcestershire sauce (or
　　Henderson's Relish)
1½ x 400g tins of lentils, plus
　　½ a tin of the liquid
1 tsp onion granules
1 tsp garlic granules
1 tsp dried oregano
a few sprigs of thyme, leaves
　　picked
sea salt and freshly ground black
　　pepper

To serve
steamed spring greens
crusty bread

1. Thinly slice your potatoes (you could use a food processor or a mandoline) and leave to soak in a large bowl of water.

2. Put the carrot and onion into your slow cooker, then pour in the stock. Add the garlic, mushrooms, tomato purée, Worcestershire sauce, lentils and their water, dried spices and fresh thyme, then season. Cook on low for 3 hours.

3. Drain the potatoes and pat dry with a clean tea towel or kitchen paper. Arrange on top of the filling in the slow cooker.

4. Pop a tea towel over the cooker, close the lid and cook for a further 2–3 hours, depending on how thick the potatoes are.

5. Serve with your favourite greens and some crusty bread and enjoy.

Sage & Mustard Pork

COOK 3 hours on high or 6 hours on low   **SERVES** 4–6

This dish is packed full of flavour. Perfect for a mid-week meal with buttery mashed potato and for even more comfort you can add some crusty bread.

1kg pork fillet, cut into similar-
    sized chunks
2 onions, finely chopped
3 carrots, finely chopped
2 sticks of celery, finely chopped
1 tsp dried sage
1 tsp dried parsley
1 bay leaf
2 tbsp wholegrain mustard
200ml cider
300ml chicken stock
2 tbsp peas
a handful of fresh sage leaves,
    chopped
sea salt and freshly ground black
    pepper

To serve
mashed potato
crusty bread (optional)

1. Heat a pan over a high heat and sear the pork for a few minutes until browned all over, then transfer to the slow cooker.

2. Add the onion, carrot and celery, along with the dried spices and mustard. Pour in the cider and chicken stock, season and stir well. Cook on high for 2 hours or low for 5 hours.

3. Add the peas and chopped fresh sage, stir, then cook for a further hour.

4. Serve with some buttery mashed potatoes and crusty bread to soak up the delicious cider gravy.

Butterbean, Pesto & Chorizo Stew

COOK 6 hours on low or 3 hours on high **SERVES** 4–6

A perfect dish for any season. When you serve up your stew, you can't help but notice
the vibrant colours in your bowl. This dish is packed full of goodness, perfect for
leftovers for lunch the next day too.

250g chorizo, chopped
2 x 400g tins of butter beans,
   drained and rinsed
2 x 400g tins of chopped
   tomatoes
1 red onion, finely sliced
1 tsp piri-piri sauce
1 tsp smoked paprika
sea salt and freshly ground black
   pepper

To serve
4–6 tbsp green pesto
100g Parmesan cheese, grated
a handful of fresh basil leaves,
   chopped
a small handful of pine nuts
a drizzle of olive oil
4–6 slices of focaccia

1. Put all the ingredients into your slow cooker, season and stir
well. Cook on low for 6 hours or high for 3 hours.

2. Serve topped with spoonfuls of pesto, scattered with grated
Parmesan, fresh basil and pine nuts, drizzled with olive oil and
alongside some tasty focaccia.

Chicken, Chorizo & Red Pepper Spicy Rice

COOK 7 hours on low or 4 hours on high   **SERVES** 4

This is an amazingly tasty meal that's perfect for mid-week. You may want to make a double batch, as I guarantee everyone will be asking for seconds.

150g chorizo, chopped

3 chicken breasts, cut into small chunks

2 tsp garlic granules

1 onion, finely chopped

1 tsp chilli flakes

1 tsp paprika

1 tsp sriracha

1 x 400g tin of chopped tomatoes

750ml chicken stock

80ml white wine

4 jarred roasted red peppers, sliced lengthways

2 x 250g packets of microwaveable rice

150g sweetcorn (frozen or tinned)

sea salt and freshly ground black pepper

To serve

a handful of fresh parsley leaves, chopped

2 tbsp red pesto

1. Put all your ingredients except the rice and sweetcorn into the slow cooker, then season and stir. Cook on low for 5 hours or high for 3 hours.

2. Add the rice and sweetcorn, stir, then cook for a further 2 hours on low or 1 hour on high.

3. Serve scattered with parsley, with a dollop of red pesto.

Stuffed Red Peppers

COOK 2 hours on high   **SERVES** 2

These are a quick and easy, mid-week favourite in my household. Healthy and light they are the perfect summer meal and are also great for customizing with your favourite ingredients.

4 large red peppers
1 x 250g packet of
    microwaveable rice
1 tbsp olive oil
1 onion, finely chopped
3 tomatoes, finely chopped
½ x 400g tin red kidney beans,
    drained and rinsed
1 tbsp dried oregano
a handful of fresh basil leaves,
    chopped
sea salt and freshly ground black
    pepper

To serve
1 tbsp balsamic vinegar
crisp green salad

1. Start by slicing the tops off the peppers and gently scooping out the insides. Set aside.

2. Make the filling by spooning the rice into a bowl, drizzling with the olive oil and breaking it up with a fork. Add the onion and tomatoes and stir well. Add the kidney beans, oregano and half the basil, then season.

3. Place your rice mixture into your prepared peppers trying not to over fill, and carefully place into your slow cooker.

4. Serve scattered with the remaining basil and drizzled with the balsamic vinegar, with a crisp salad on the side.

Tarragon Chicken

COOK 4 hours on high or 7 hours on low   **SERVES** 4–6

As well as costing you less, chicken thighs are packed with flavour which makes them perfect for the slow cooker. This is a truly delicious family recipe.

700g boneless, skinless chicken thighs

2 cloves of garlic, crushed

6 shallots, sliced

200g Chantenay carrots (make sure they're all a similar size – cut in half if not)

½ x 400g tin of cannellini beans, drained and rinsed

1 tsp dried tarragon

1 tsp dried parsley

350ml chicken stock

1 tsp cornflour

1 tbsp cold water

3 tbsp crème fraîche

1–2 tbsp Dijon mustard

sea salt and freshly ground black pepper

To serve

a handful of fresh tarragon leaves, chopped

mashed potato

steamed spring greens

1. Place the chicken thighs in your slow cooker, add the garlic and season. Scatter over the sliced shallot, carrots, cannellini beans and the dried herbs, then pour over the chicken stock. Cook on high for 4 hours or low for 7 hours.

2. An hour before the end of the cooking time, mix the cornflour to a paste with the water, then add to the slow cooker. This will help to create a slightly thicker sauce.

3. When the chicken is cooked, lift the thighs out of the sauce and leave to rest for 10 minutes before serving.

4. Add the crème fraîche and mustard to the sauce, stirring well, then pour the sauce over the chicken.

5. Serve sprinkled with fresh tarragon, with some buttery mashed potato and your favourite steamed greens on the side.

Spicy Chicken Drumsticks

COOK 6 hours on low, and overnight marinating   **SERVES** 4

Spicy, sticky and messy! This is ideal family-night-in-front-of-the-TV food.

1 tbsp sriracha

2 tsp piri-piri rub

1 tbsp pesto

2 tsp paprika

1 tsp garlic granules

1 tbsp tomato ketchup

8 chicken drumsticks

sea salt and freshly ground black
pepper

To serve

1 red chilli, finely chopped

a handful of fresh coriander
leaves

4 handfuls of oven chips, cooked
from frozen

4 corn on the cob

1. In a large airtight container, mix all the ingredients except the chicken together to make a marinade. Add the chicken and marinate overnight in the fridge.

2. The next day, all you need to do is transfer the drumsticks to your slow cooker, season, then cook on low for 6 hours, turning halfway.

3. Serve scattered with fresh chilli and coriander, with some chips and corn on the cob on the side.

Tandoori Chicken Wraps

COOK 6 hours on low or 3 hours on high   **SERVES** 4

This is one of my go-to mid-week meals – the flavours are so fresh, and there's zero prep to do. The tandoori rub makes more than you'll need but it's great to have to hand for when you want to make these wraps again!

2 large onions, sliced

2 tbsp olive oil

4 chicken breasts

½ iceberg lettuce

1 cucumber

a handful of fresh mint

175g Greek yoghurt

4 naan breads

sea salt and freshly ground
    black pepper

For the tandoori rub

1 tsp ground coriander

1 tsp ground cumin

1 tsp garlic granules

1 tsp ground ginger

1 tsp cayenne pepper

1 tsp garam masala

½ tsp ground cloves

½ tsp ground fenugreek

½ tsp ground cinnamon

½ tsp ground cardamom

sea salt and freshly ground black
    pepper

1. First, make the tandoori rub by mixing all the ingredients together in a bowl. Use 2 tablespoons for this recipe and store the rest in an airtight container.

2. Arrange the sliced onion to cover the bottom of your slow cooker. In a small bowl, mix the 2 tablespoons of the tandoori rub with the olive oil, season, then cover the chicken breasts. Place on top of your onion. Cook on low for 6 hours or high for 3 hours.

3. Meanwhile, shred the lettuce, finely chop the cucumber and rinse and chop the mint. Mix the mint with the yoghurt and set everything aside in the fridge.

4. When your chicken is cooked, leave to rest for 10 minutes, then slice.

5. Create your wraps by dividing the sliced chicken among the naan breads, spooning over some of the mint yoghurt, scattering over some lettuce and cucumber, then rolling up.

Paprika Chicken

COOK 4–5 hours on low   **SERVES** 4

This recipe could not be easier. You can also prepare this ahead of time by marinating the chicken in the fridge overnight. I serve mine with brown rice and a dollop of Greek yoghurt. So simple, yet so tasty.

4 chicken breasts, sliced
1 x 400g tin of chopped
    tomatoes
1 heaped tsp paprika
1 tsp dried oregano
1 tsp nduja paste
2 tbsp red pesto
1 large onion, chopped
2 cloves of garlic, crushed
1 carrot, grated
8 slices of chorizo
150ml chicken stock
a handful of fresh spinach or
    1 nugget of frozen
sea salt and freshly ground black
    pepper

To serve
brown rice
Greek yoghurt

1. Start by placing the chicken strips in your slow cooker. Add the rest of the ingredients except the spinach, season, stir and cook for 3 hours on low.

2. Add the spinach, stir, then cook for a further hour.

3. Check that the chicken is cooked through with no trace of pink (cook for a further hour if so), season to taste, and there you have it – it really is that simple!

4. Serve with brown rice and Greek yoghurt.

Perfect Mid-Week Beef Stew

COOK 6–7 hours on low   **SERVES** 4

A mid-week wonder. This stew is super easy, and you can also freeze any leftovers for when time is just not on your side – which happens to me all too often!

2 tbsp cornflour

1kg shin of beef, cut into
   bite-sized pieces

2 tsp dried Italian herbs

1 litre beef stock

1 Oxo cube, crumbled

1 tbsp beef gravy granules

2 large onions, chopped

2 large carrots, chopped

2 cloves of garlic, crushed

2 tbsp Worcestershire sauce

2 tbsp tomato ketchup

sea salt and freshly ground black
   pepper

To serve

mashed potato

bread rolls

1. Start by putting the cornflour into a large bowl, then add the beef and toss to coat. Add a little salt and pepper and 1 teaspoon of the Italian herbs.

2. Heat a pan over a high heat, then sear the beef for around 5 minutes until browned on all sides (you can leave this step out if you wish). Transfer the beef to the slow cooker.

3. Mix the stock, Oxo cube and gravy granules, then pour over the beef. Add the onion, carrot, garlic, the rest of the Italian herbs, the Worcestershire sauce and ketchup. Give it a stir and cook on low for 6–7 hours, stirring occasionally.

4. Season to taste and serve with some buttery mashed potato and crusty bread rolls for mopping up the sauce.

Fragrant Chickpea Curry with Lemon & Coriander Rice

COOK 4 hours on low **SERVES** 4

This dish is so vibrant and healthy and it's completely delicious. A perfect dinner for meat-free Mondays. It's another great one to prepare the day before and leave in the fridge, ready to pop in the slow cooker in the morning. You can also leave out the chillies if you don't like it too hot.

2 onions, chopped

4 large tomatoes, chopped

500ml vegetable stock

4 cloves of garlic, crushed

2 x 400g tins of chickpeas, drained and rinsed

1 x 400g tin of chopped tomatoes

100ml coconut cream

2 tsp paprika

2 tbsp curry powder

1 tsp ground coriander

1–2 dried red chillies

1 star anise

2 tbsp mango chutney

200–300g basmati rice or 1 x 250g packet of microwaveable rice

zest of 1 lemon

a handful of fresh coriander leaves, chopped, plus extra to serve

sea salt and freshly ground black pepper

1. Put the onion and tomatoes into your slow cooker. Pour in the stock, add the garlic, chickpeas, tinned tomatoes, coconut cream, spices, chilli and mango chutney and stir. Cook on low for 4 hours.

2. Towards the end of the cooking time, cook the rice as per the packet instructions. Mix with the lemon zest and chopped coriander.

3. Just before serving, remove the chillies from the curry, season well to taste and serve with the lemon and coriander rice.

Salmon & Orzo Pasta

COOK 1 ½–2 hours, then 30 minutes on high   **SERVES** 4

Honestly, this is the most delicious pasta I have ever cooked in my slow cooker. It's just the right amount of perfect.

4 skinless salmon fillets
500g tomato passata
350ml vegetable stock
350g orzo
1 tsp paprika
1 tsp garlic granules
1 tsp dried oregano
5 sun-dried tomatoes
2 tbsp red pesto
sea salt and freshly ground black
    pepper

To serve
a handful of Parmesan shavings
garlic bread
a handful of fresh parsley leaves,
    chopped

1. Preheat your slow cooker on low for 10 minutes.

2. Put the salmon fillets and passata into the slow cooker, then pour in the vegetable stock. Cook on low for 2–3 hours (the time will depend on the size of your fillets).

3. Add the orzo, paprika, garlic granules, oregano, sun-dried tomatoes and pesto. Season, stir, then cook on high for 30 minutes, stirring a few times throughout.

4. Serve sprinkled with Parmesan, with some garlic bread on the side. I like to add a little chopped parsley, too.

Thai-Style Fish Parcels

COOK 2 hours on high   **SERVES** 2

I serve mine with green beans and asparagus, but it's also delicious with sugar snap peas and broccoli, or why not try mixed peppers and pak choi. Use whatever vegetables you prefer – making it your own is what cooking is all about. If you like it spicy, add another chilli to serve.

1 lemon, sliced

a bunch of fresh coriander

1 red chilli, thinly sliced

thumb-sized piece of fresh ginger, grated

2 sticks of lemongrass, bashed

2 cod fillets

1 tbsp soy sauce

1 tsp sesame oil

2 cloves of garlic, thinly sliced

a handful of green beans (about 10–15), trimmed

a bunch of asparagus

sea salt and freshly ground black pepper

To serve
rice or noodles

1. I like to use baking paper for this, but you can use tinfoil, too. Make 2 parcels with baking paper/foil that fit snugly into your slow cooker. Arrange the lemon slices, coriander, chilli, ginger and lemongrass stalks in the parcels and place the fish on top.

2. In a small bowl, mix together the soy sauce, sesame oil, garlic and a pinch of pepper, then pour this over the fish. Bring the sides of the parcels together to seal, then place in your slow cooker and cook on high for 2 hours. Let the slow cooker do its magic.

3. Add the greens about 30–45 minutes before the end of the cooking time, placing them around your parcels. Alternatively, you can cook them in your air fryer at 180°C for 3–5 minutes.

4. Serve with rice or noodles.

Jacket Potatoes 4 Ways

COOK 4 hours on high or 8 hours on low   **SERVES** 4

Who doesn't love a jacket potato! It's my go-to lunch any day of the week, especially when I found out you could cook them in the slow cooker. It has made lunchtimes, particularly in the school holidays, so much easier. I set my slow cooker when we get up in the morning, et voilà, lunch is already sorted! I've suggested some of my family's favourite toppings here but the possibilities are endless – and it's such a great way to use up any leftovers.

4 baking potatoes
2 tbsp olive oil
sea salt and freshly
    ground black pepper

1. Carefully prick the potatoes with a fork or sharp knife, then brush on the olive oil and season well. Wrap the potatoes in tinfoil and place in your slow cooker. Cook on high for 4 hours or low for 8. You may need to adjust the times depending on the size of the potatoes.

2. Check with a knife to make sure the potatoes are soft throughout. If you like a more crispy skin, why not finish them off in the air fryer for 3–4 minutes at 190°C, or in a preheated oven at 190°C/375°F/gas 5 for for 10 minutes.

Serving suggestions/Toppings

* My Homemade Baked Beans (see page 40) and a sprinkle of grated Cheddar cheese

* My Chilli Con Carne (see page 62) with a spoonful of sour cream and chopped coriander

* Soft cream cheese with smoked salmon and a squeeze of lemon and chopped chives

* Chopped chorizo with torn mozzarella, sun-dried tomatoes and fresh basil

Weekend
Wonders

Cheese Fondue

COOK 1 hour on high   **SERVES** 6 as a starter

A great recipe for sharing with friends and family. There's nothing better than having a huge bowl of this cheese fondue in the middle of your dining table so you can all get stuck in!

200g mature Cheddar cheese, grated
200g Gruyère cheese, grated
150g Gouda cheese, grated
2 tbsp cider vinegar
1 tsp cornflour
1 tsp cayenne pepper
2 tbsp crème fraîche

To serve
selection of toasted breads, cut into bite-sized pieces
baby corn
sliced or baby carrots
sticks of celery

1. Preheat your slow cooker on high for 5 minutes.

2. Put the cheeses into your slow cooker. Mix the vinegar and cornflour together, give it a little whisk, then add to the slow cooker. Cook on high for 1 hour.

3. After cooking, season the fondue with the cayenne pepper, giving it a little whisk. Add the crème fraîche 15 minutes before serving, stirring well.

4. Serve with a selection of toasted breads and crudités.

Asian-Style Pork

COOK 3–4 hours on high   **SERVES** 4

It wasn't until I was in my mid-twenties that I truly appreciated the fantastic flavour of pork and I started to experiment more when cooking it for myself. My son and I absolutely adore this dish and I hope you all will too.

1 onion, sliced
700g boneless pork shoulder
1 tbsp ground ginger
2 tsp garlic granules
400ml vegetable stock
3 tbsp runny honey
1 tbsp sesame oil
1 tsp light soy sauce
3 tbsp oyster sauce
2 tbsp tomato ketchup
1 tbsp cornflour
sea salt and freshly ground black
    pepper

To serve
1 red chilli, finely chopped
sesame seeds
rice

1. Put the sliced onion into your slow cooker and place the pork shoulder on top.

2. In a bowl, mix together the rest of the ingredients except the cornflour, then pour this sauce over the pork. Season, then cook on high for 3–4 hours, turning at least twice throughout.

3. After cooking, remove the pork and leave to rest for 15 minutes.

4. Meanwhile, mix the cornflour with a splash of water in a mug or small bowl until you get a thick paste. Add this to the sauce in the slow cooker and set to 'reduce' to thicken it.

5. Once the pork has rested, shred with 2 forks and add back to the now thickened sauce.

6. Serve sprinkled with chopped fresh chilli and sesame seeds, with a side of rice.

Beef Brisket

COOK 6–7 hours on high **SERVES** 6

A super-delicious treat for the weekend. The meat just falls apart! Perfect served in a toasted brioche bun with crispy lettuce and homemade coleslaw on the side.

1kg beef brisket
450ml beef stock
1 large onion, chopped
1 clove of garlic, crushed
1 tbsp Worcestershire sauce
1 tsp Bovril
1 tbsp tomato ketchup
sea salt and freshly ground black
   pepper

To serve
6 brioche buns, toasted
lettuce leaves
Crunchy Slaw (see page 160)

1. Heat a non-stick frying pan over a high heat, then add the beef and sear on all sides until browned.

2. Put all the other ingredients into your slow cooker, add the beef and season. Cook on high for 6–7 hours, stirring occasionally.

3. Once cooked, shred the brisket using two forks.

4. Serve in a brioche bun with some crispy lettuce, and homemade slaw on the side.

Sticky Ribs

COOK 8 hours on low   **SERVES** 4

I've tried many a rib recipe over the years, but this is my favourite. I just love the combination of sweet and sour flavours; it's the perfect amount of both. You may need to adjust the time as well as the amount of apple juice for this dish, depending on the size of the ribs. If you need to add more, please do so!

1.5kg pork spare ribs
300ml apple juice
1 tsp paprika
sea salt and freshly ground black
   pepper

For the BBQ sauce

250g brown sauce
250g tomato ketchup
100g wholegrain mustard
125ml Worcestershire sauce
100ml whisky
3 tbsp runny honey
dash of Tabasco sauce

To serve

4 corn on the cob
Crunchy Slaw (see page 160)
4 large handfuls of sweet potato
   fries, cooked from frozen

1. In a bowl, mix together all the ingredients for your BBQ sauce and set aside. Season the ribs and brush them with half of your BBQ sauce.

2. Pour 150ml of the apple juice into the bottom of your slow cooker, then add the ribs. Cook for 8 hours on low. Depending on the amount of meat on the ribs, you may need to adjust the time. Turn them over from time to time in the sauce to make sure they don't dry out.

3. After 8 hours, carefully transfer the ribs from the slow cooker to a serving plate and drizzle with the sauce.

4. Serve with corn on the cob, homemade slaw and sweet potato fries.

Piri-Piri Chicken

COOK 6–7 hours on low, and overnight marinating **SERVES** 4

This is a great recipe for an easy Saturday night dinner. We serve this in wraps, with a big bowl of salad and an array of dips. Let everyone get stuck in and help themselves. To make this dish vegetarian, simply use large mushrooms instead of the chicken and halve the cooking time.

4 chicken breasts

3 mixed peppers, deseeded and chopped into large chunks

2 onions, chopped into large chunks

sea salt and freshly ground black pepper

For the marinade

1 chicken stock cube, crumbled

1 tbsp olive oil

1 tsp paprika

1 tsp piri-piri rub

½ tsp chilli powder

1 tsp garlic granules

To serve

4–8 tortilla wraps

chopped fresh coriander leaves

1 red chilli, chopped (optional)

salad

sour cream

guacamole

1. First, make the marinade paste by simply mixing all the ingredients together in a small cup or bowl. If it needs thinning out a little, add a small splash of water. Mix well and spread over your chicken breasts. Leave in an airtight container overnight in the fridge ready to use the next day. I find this really intensifies the flavours.

2. Put the marinated chicken into your slow cooker and cook on low for 3 hours. Stir well, add the peppers and onion, season, then cook for a further 3 hours. Check the chicken – you might need to cook it for another 30 minutes–1 hour depending on the size of your chicken breasts.

3. Serve in wraps with a sprinkle of fresh coriander and some chopped fresh chilli if you like spice, with salad, sour cream and guacamole.

Whole Chicken Cooked in Cider

COOK 4–5 hours on low (depending on the size of your chicken)   **SERVES** 4

I just love the combination of chicken, cider, lettuce and leeks; they marry together so well. Just thinking about this creamy sauce makes me hungry! A perfect Sunday lunch alternative that everyone will enjoy.

3 shallots, sliced

1–2 leeks, sliced

3 x 300ml cans of cider

1 small to medium chicken (about 1.2kg – make sure it fits into your slow cooker)

4 little gem lettuces, sliced lengthways into quarters

100ml single cream

a few sprigs of fresh rosemary, leaves picked

sea salt and freshly ground black pepper

To serve

Rosemary Roast Potatoes (see page 154) or mashed potatoes

crusty bread

1. I like to preheat my slow cooker for this recipe on low for about 30 minutes.

2. Put the shallot and leek into the slow cooker, then pour in the cider. Add the chicken, breast side down to begin with, turning it halfway through cooking. Cook for 3 hours on low.

3. Add the lettuce quarters, placing them around the chicken, which is now breast side up. Cook for a further 1–2 hours, making sure the chicken is cooked through with no trace of pink. Remove the chicken and leave to rest for 10 minutes.

4. Meanwhile, make a delicious sauce by putting the single cream and rosemary leaves into the slow cooker. Season, then turn the heat up to high and keep stirring for 10 minutes or so.

5. Carve the chicken, divide among your plates, then pour over the sauce.

6. Serve with roast potatoes or buttery mash, and don't forget some crusty bread to mop up the creamy sauce.

Simple Fish Curry

COOK 2 hours on low **SERVES** 4

A real winning curry – it's easy to prepare and so fresh and vibrant in colour. This is one of the best summer dishes I make in my slow cooker. It's not just for wintertime!

750g skinless white fish, cut into
   chunks
2 heaped tsp curry powder
1 tsp ground turmeric
4 cloves of garlic, crushed
thumb-sized piece of fresh ginger,
   peeled and grated
250ml vegetable stock
250g fresh spinach
100ml tinned coconut milk
3 tbsp plain yoghurt
a handful of fresh coriander
   leaves
1 red chilli, finely sliced
sea salt and freshly ground black
   pepper

To serve
basmati rice
naan bread

1. Place the fish in your slow cooker. Scatter over the spices, garlic and ginger, then pour in the stock. Cook on low for 1 hour.

2. Add the spinach and coconut milk, then cook for a further hour.

3. Check the fish to make sure it's cooked through (if your fish is in bigger chunks you may need to cook it for a little longer), then stir in the yoghurt and scatter over the coriander and chopped chilli. Season to taste.

4. Serve with basmati rice and naan bread.

Red Thai Prawn Noodles

COOK 4 hours on low **SERVES** 4

This is such a versatile dish – you can easily adjust it to your preferred flavours! Feel free to add whatever vegetables you have in the fridge. I love to use peppers in this dish, but you could also use sugar snap peas, broccoli, spinach or even asparagus – the list is endless. I use frozen prawns, but you could use fresh prawns, too.

500g frozen prawns

4 tbsp red Thai curry paste

1 x 400ml tin of coconut milk

3 kaffir lime leaves

2 dried red chillies (leave out if you don't like spice)

2 red peppers, deseeded and thinly sliced

200g dried egg noodles

1 pak choi, quartered

sea salt and freshly ground black pepper

To serve

a handful of fresh coriander leaves, chopped

a handful of pistachios, roughly chopped

1. Put the prawns, red Thai curry paste, coconut milk, kaffir lime leaves and red chillies, if using, into your slow cooker. Season, stir, then cook on low for 2 hours.

2. Add the sliced peppers and cook for a further 30 minutes.

3. Meanwhile, cook the noodles according to the pack instructions, then drain, run them under cold water and set aside.

4. Add the pak choi and noodles to the slow cooker, stir, then cook for a final 30 minutes.

5. Season to taste and serve sprinkled with fresh coriander and pistachios.

Beef Short Ribs

COOK 6–7 hours on low   **SERVES** 2

This recipe is ideal for a low and slow cook. The combination of flavours works perfectly, and the beef ends up so succulent, it will just fall off the bone.

4 beef short ribs
1 carrot, chopped
1 stick of celery, chopped
1 onion, chopped
1 tbsp Worcestershire sauce
1 beef stock cube, crumbled
575ml beef stock
2 tbsp tomato purée
1 tsp garlic paste (shop bought or
    you can make your own by
    crushing and mashing 3 cloves
    of garlic)
1 tsp cayenne pepper
sea salt and freshly ground black
    pepper

To serve
salad
2 large handfuls of oven chips,
    cooked from frozen
2 corn on the cob

1. I like to start by searing the beef ribs in a hot pan for around 5 minutes until browned on all sides, but this is an optional step.

2. Put the carrot, celery and onion into your slow cooker, then place the beef on top. Mix the rest of the ingredients in a large mixing bowl until well combined, then pour over the beef. Season, then cook on low for 6–7 hours, turning the beef a few times throughout and spooning the gravy over the ribs at the same time.

3. Serve with a side salad, chips and some buttered corn on the cob.

Mongolian Beef Curry

COOK 6 hours on low   **SERVES** 4

This dish has the perfect Saturday takeaway vibe. If you don't like it too spicy, leave out the sriracha; if you love spice, why not add a chopped fresh chilli to garnish! I like to use rump steak, but please do experiment and feel free to use whatever beef cut you prefer.

1kg rump steak
1 heaped tbsp cornflour
1 heaped tbsp brown sugar
3 cloves of garlic, crushed
thumb-sized piece of fresh ginger,
    peeled and grated
3 heaped tbsp light soy sauce
1 tbsp sriracha (depending on
    how hot you like it)
1 tsp sesame oil
2 tbsp hoisin sauce
1 large carrot, grated
200ml water
sea salt and freshly ground black
    pepper

To serve

4 spring onions, shredded
a handful of unsalted peanuts,
    crushed
2 tbsp sesame seeds
long grain rice

1. Slice your steak into similar-sized pieces and toss with the cornflour, making sure to coat each piece.

2. Put the sugar, garlic, ginger, soy sauce, sriracha, sesame oil and hoisin sauce into your slow cooker and stir. Add the beef, season and cook on low for 4 hours.

3. Add the grated carrot and stir. If at this point you feel you need to add a dash more water, do so. Cook for a further 2 hours.

4. Serve scattered with spring onions, crushed nuts and sesame seeds, with a side of rice.

Honey and Hoisin Duck Wraps

COOK 8 hours on low **SERVES** 2

This is hands down my son's favourite recipe. We tried duck wraps at a festival once and loved them so much, I just had to try and recreate them at home. The duck cooks so well in the slow cooker; the tender, juicy meat just falls off the bone.

1 large onion, sliced

2 duck legs

3 tbsp soy sauce

½ tsp Chinese five spice

1 tbsp runny honey

1 tbsp brown sugar

1 tsp garlic granules

1 tsp sesame oil

2 large flour tortillas or 4 small

5 spring onions, sliced into
    matchsticks

¼ cucumber, sliced into
    matchsticks or shredded

½ bag of lamb's lettuce

3–4 tbsp hoisin sauce

1. Put the onion into your slow cooker. Pat dry the duck legs with kitchen paper, then place them on top of the onion.

2. In a bowl, mix together the soy sauce, five spice, honey, brown sugar, garlic granules and sesame oil. Brush onto your duck legs, then cook on low for 8 hours.

3. When the duck legs have finished cooking, you can finish them off in a preheated oven at 200°C /400°F/gas 6 for 8–10 minutes, or in the air fryer for 5 minutes at 200°C, if you want super-crispy skin!

4. Shred the duck and divide between the tortillas. Add the spring onion and cucumber and some lamb's lettuce. Drizzle over the hoisin sauce, then roll them up. Serve with some chunky chips.

Brunch Boats

COOK 2 hours on high   **SERVES** 4

These are such a treat for a lazy Sunday brunch. You can mix it up with your fillings – try adding some cooked bacon or chorizo or even some spinach. This dish is so versatile and a great way to use up the odds and ends from your fridge. Why not add a side of my homemade Baked Beans (see page 40) too?

a drizzle of oil

12 eggs

200ml whole milk

1 tsp dried parsley

4 taco shells

4 mushrooms, sliced

5 vine tomatoes, sliced

a handful of grated Cheddar cheese

sea salt and freshly ground black pepper

To serve

a handful of fresh parsley leaves

1. First, drizzle a little oil into your slow cooker, so the boats don't stick to the bottom.

2. In a large bowl, whisk the eggs and milk together, add the dried parsley and season. Carefully pour this mixture into the taco shells, but don't overfill them. Divide the sliced mushrooms and tomatoes among the boats, then sprinkle the Cheddar on top. Carefully place the boats inside your slow cooker and cook on high for 2 hours.

3. Serve with a good grind of black pepper and a sprinkle of chopped parsley.

Red Thai Whole Chicken

COOK 6–7 hours on low   **SERVES** 4

This is such a tasty dish with just the right amount of kick. My family loves this chicken with steamed green beans, but you could also try basmati rice and pan-fried mixed peppers.

1 small to medium chicken (about 1.2kg – make sure it fits into your slow cooker)

For the sauce
1 stick of lemongrass
1 tsp fish sauce
thumb-sized piece of fresh ginger, peeled and grated
250ml chicken stock
1 x 400ml tin of coconut milk
3 tbsp red Thai curry paste
3 cloves of garlic, crushed
4 lime leaves
a squeeze of lime juice
1 tsp brown sugar
a handful of fresh coriander leaves, plus a few extra to serve
1 red chilli, finely chopped
5 Thai basil leaves
sea salt and freshly ground black pepper

To serve
basmati rice
steamed green beans
pan-fried mixed peppers

1. Put all the sauce ingredients, except the coriander, chilli and Thai basil, into a saucepan over a medium heat, season and cook for about 5 minutes, stirring until the sugar dissolves.

2. Place the chicken in your slow cooker and pour over the sauce. Cook on high for 6 hours. During cooking, occasionally baste the chicken with the sauce.

3. Check that the chicken is cooked through with no trace of pink (you may need to cook it for a further hour depending on the size), then leave to rest for 15 minutes before carving.

4. Add the coriander, chilli and Thai basil leaves to the sauce in the slow cooker and stir.

5. Carve your chicken, arrange on a serving plate and pour over the sauce.

6. Serve with a sprinkle of fresh coriander, with a side of rice and garlic naans to soak up all the flavour.

Green Thai Chicken Curry

COOK 3 hours on high or 5–6 hours on low **SERVES** 4

Perfect for a 'takeaway-night'; it's less expensive than an actual takeaway and super delicious. Over the years I have tried and tested so many ways to make green Thai curry paste. I finally think I've found the one! You can store the paste in an airtight jar for up to 2 weeks, too, so it's ideal if you want to be prepared and make it ahead of time.

4 chicken breasts, sliced into
   strips
1 x 400ml tin of coconut milk
sea salt and freshly ground black
   pepper

For the curry paste

3 green chillies
2 sticks of lemongrass, bashed
   and roughly chopped
6 lime leaves
6 spring onions, chopped
2 cloves of garlic
thumb-sized piece of fresh ginger,
   peeled and chopped
zest and juice of 1 lemon
1 small bunch of fresh coriander
a handful of fresh Thai basil leaves
1 tsp sesame oil
½ tsp chilli powder
½ tsp garlic granules
½ tsp ground turmeric
½ tsp ground cumin

To serve

a handful of crushed pistachios
a handful of fresh coriander leaves
basmati rice
red chilli, sliced

1. Blitz all the ingredients for the curry paste together in a food processor or a blender, adding a splash of water to loosen it if you need to. I like to use the paste to marinate my chicken in the fridge for a few hours before cooking, but this is optional.

2. Put the chicken, coconut milk and curry paste into your slow cooker. Season, then cook on high for 3 hours or low for 5–6 hours. Stir a few times while cooking and season well.

3. Serve sprinkled with pistachio nuts and fresh coriander, with a side of basmati rice.

Doner Kebab

COOK 6 hours on low   **SERVES** 4

I don't know about you but, for me, sometimes there's nothing like a doner kebab on a Friday night! Let's face it, takeaways are not getting any cheaper with the cost of living rising, so I created my version of a doner, and I haven't looked back since. I tend to go heavy on the salad with lashing of garlic mayo.

750g minced lamb or beef
1 tsp ground turmeric
1 tsp garlic granules
1 tsp onion granules
1 tsp nduja paste
1 tsp paprika
2 tsp ground cumin
1 tbsp vegetable oil
sea salt and freshly ground black
    pepper

To serve

4 pittas, toasted
salad
Crunchy Slaw (see page 160)
Yoghurt & Mint Raita (see page
    160) or garlic mayonnaise
4 large handfuls of sweet potato
    fries, cooked from frozen

1. Put all the ingredients into a food processor, season, then pulse until well combined.

2. Brush a large piece of tinfoil with vegetable oil, place your kebab mixture in the centre and shape it into a large sausage, not too big so it doesn't fit into your slow cooker. Wrap the mixture tightly in the foil and seal the ends. Place this into your slow cooker and cook on low for 6 hours.

3. When finished, open the foil and baste the kebab with the juices in the bottom – this is important, as it will absorb all the flavours. Thinly slice and serve in toasted pitta breads, with salad, homemade slaw and raita. And why not add some sweet potato fries on the side?

Easy-Peasy Pizza

COOK 2 hours on high   **SERVES** 1

Now, you may be thinking, why do I need to put a pizza in the slow cooker when it doesn't take long in the oven? This recipe is perfect for when I'm busy in the evening and want to have something ready to eat when I get home. I use ready-made pizza dough, but of course you can make your own.

1 ready-made pizza base
1 tbsp tomato purée
1 tsp dried oregano
a handful of grated mozzarella
    cheese
4–6 slices of chorizo
6 olives, pitted and sliced

To serve
a drizzle of chilli oil
salad

1. Line your slow cooker with baking paper and place your pizza base in the bottom with the edges slightly rolled up. Spread over the tomato purée, sprinkle on the oregano and mozzarella, then top with the chorizo and olives. Cook on high for 2 hours.

2. Serve with a drizzle of chilli oil and a salad on the side.

Chicken Curry

COOK 5–6 hours on low   **SERVES** 4

This is a mild curry, so it's perfect for kids too! I marinate my chicken overnight in the fridge with all the spices. I want to make life as easy as I can, so any prep I can do the day before is a winner for me! However, it's not necessary if you don't have the time.

1 white onion, finely chopped

450ml chicken stock

500g boneless, skinless chicken thighs, cut into small bite-sized pieces

3 cloves of garlic, grated

thumb-sized piece of fresh ginger, peeled and grated

2 tsp ground turmeric

2 tbsp garam masala

½ tsp chilli powder

70g tomato purée

8–10 cherry tomatoes, halved

100g single or double cream (optional)

sea salt and freshly ground black pepper

To serve

basmati rice

your favourite breads (naan, etc.)

1. I like to preheat my slow cooker for this recipe on low for 30 minutes, but it's not necessary.

2. Put the onion into the slow cooker, pour in the stock and give them a stir. Add the chicken, garlic, ginger and spices, then stir again well. Add the tomato purée and cherry tomatoes and season. Marinate overnight if you have the time. Cook for 5–6 hours on low, adding the cream 30 minutes before the end.

3. Serve with basmati rice and your favourite breads.

Zingy Beef Tacos

COOK 7 hours on low   **SERVES** 4

I love the fact that you can make this recipe your own. You can use more or less spice, or use minced lamb or pork instead of beef. Feel free to mix up the toppings, too. It's a great sharing meal for the whole family without the stress. Get stuck in!

1 large red onion, finely chopped
2 mixed peppers, deseeded and
    finely chopped
2 sticks of celery, finely chopped
2 small carrots, grated
1 tsp ground cumin
1 tsp onion granules
1 tsp garlic granules
½ tsp ground turmeric
1 tsp paprika
1 tsp piri-piri rub
750g lean minced beef
100ml water
sea salt and freshly ground black
    pepper

To serve
12 taco shells
a handful of fresh coriander
    leaves
1 lime, quartered
½ iceberg lettuce, shredded
grated Cheddar cheese
guacamole
pickled red onions
1 red chilli, sliced

1. Put all the ingredients into your slow cooker, season and stir well. Cook on low for 7 hours.

2. Serve in taco shells, with fresh coriander, a squeeze of lime juice and your selection of toppings.

Soups, Sides & Sauces

Chicken Soup for the Soul

COOK 8 hours on low   **SERVES** 4–6

This is my go-to recipe if I'm feeling a little under the weather. There's something about it that is just so comforting. It also freezes well, so you can have a little pick-me-up to hand for whenever you need it.

8 boneless, skinless chicken thighs, cut into small chunks
2 litres chicken stock
1 onion, finely chopped
2 sticks of celery, finely chopped
2 carrots, finely chopped
1 bay leaf
1 x 200g tin of sweetcorn, drained and rinsed
sea salt and freshly ground black pepper

To serve
a handful of fresh parsley leaves, chopped
crusty bread

1. Put all your ingredients, apart from the sweetcorn, into your slow cooker, then season and stir well. Cook on low for 7 hours.

2. Add the sweetcorn and cook for a further hour.

3. Serve scattered with fresh parsley, with some buttered crusty bread on the side.

Chickpea, Leek & Potato Soup

COOK 3 hours on high   **SERVES** 4

Comfort in a bowl. Perfect after a long day or when the weather starts to turn chillier.

1 x 400g tin of chickpeas, plus the
  liquid in the tin
2 potatoes, peeled and cut into
  cubes
2 shallots, thinly sliced
2 leeks, sliced
1 carrot, finely chopped
1 tsp dried chives
2 cloves of garlic, crushed
900ml vegetable stock
sea salt and freshly ground black
  pepper

To serve
crusty bread
olive oil

1. Put all the ingredients into your slow cooker and season well. Cook on high for 3 hours.

2. Using a hand blender, blitz the soup until smooth or if you like, you can keep it chunky.

3. Serve with some crusty bread and a drizzle of olive oil.

Mushroom & Truffle Soup

COOK 3 hours on low **SERVES** 2

Why not make a batch at the start of the week – it keeps in the fridge for up to 5 days and you could even freeze it if you make too much. If you don't like truffle oil, leave it out. I totally understand; it's not everyone's cup of tea and I know it's not a staple store-cupboard ingredient. Add a little more sage instead and it will still be super yummy! Why not try it with some air-fried/pan-fried croutons on top, too?

300g closed cup mushrooms, sliced
1 large carrot, finely chopped
2 shallots, thinly sliced
1 stick of celery, finely chopped
575ml vegetable stock
2 cloves of garlic, crushed
1 tsp dried sage
1 tsp onion granules
1–2 tsp cornflour (if you want the soup thicker)
1–2 tsp truffle oil
sea salt and freshly ground black pepper

To serve
crusty bread
a handful of fresh parsley leaves, chopped
Parmesan croutons (see page 149, optional)

1. Put the mushrooms, carrot, shallot and celery into your slow cooker. Pour in the stock. Add the garlic, sage and onion granules and stir. Cook on low for 2 hours 30 minutes.

2. After the cooking time, if, like me, you like your soup a little thicker in texture, mix the cornflour with a splash of water in a mug or small bowl, then add this to your soup along with the truffle oil. Season, then cook for a final 30 minutes.

3. Serve with some warm crusty bread, a sprinkle of parsley on top and some crispy croutons, if you like.

Soups, Sides & Sauces

Broccoli & Stilton Soup with Bacon Toast

COOK 3 hours on low   **SERVES** 4–6

The perfect winter warmer. I try to prepare mine the night before so all I need to do is pop the slow cooker on in the morning, and it's ready for lunchtime after a long dog walk. Just what you need to warm those bones on a cold winter's day. It's delicious served with bacon toasts, but these are optional – it holds its own when served simply with some crusty bread.

1 head of broccoli, cut into florets and stalk sliced
1 large white onion, chopped
1 carrot, grated
1 large leek, sliced
1 litre vegetable stock
a large knob of butter
200g Stilton cheese, crumbled
270ml single cream
sea salt and freshly ground black pepper

For the bacon toasts

8 slices of streaky bacon
4 slices of white bread
a large knob of butter

1. Put all the vegetables into your slow cooker, then pour in the stock. Cook on low for 2 hours 30 minutes.

2. Add the butter, then season with salt and plenty of pepper. I like to blend my soup, so transfer to a food processor and blend until smooth. Pour it back into your slow cooker, add the cream, crumble in the Stilton cheese, then give it a stir. Cook for a final 30 minutes.

3. Meanwhile, make the toasts. Cook the bacon in an air fryer at 180°C for 5 minutes, turning halfway, or in the oven at 180°C/350°F/gas 4 for around 15 minutes. Remove and place on kitchen paper to absorb any excess fat. Toast the bread, butter the slices and cut in half into triangles. Cut the bacon slices in half and arrange on top.

4. Serve the scrumptious soup in bowls alongside the bacon toasties to dunk in.

5. The soup will keep in the fridge for 3–4 days in an airtight container. Alternatively, keep in the fridge overnight, then freeze for up to 3 months.

Tomato & Basil Soup with Parmesan Croutons

COOK 3–4 hours on low   **SERVES** 6

This is one of my all-time favourite soups. As a child it would be my food of choice when we came back from holiday. There's just something about it that feels like home.

850g vine-ripened tomatoes, quartered
500ml vegetable stock
1 tbsp red pesto
1 large red onion, sliced
2 cloves of garlic, crushed
1 tbsp Worcestershire sauce
a handful of fresh basil leaves
sea salt and freshly ground black pepper

For the Parmesan croutons
½ baguette
1 tbsp olive oil
a handful of grated Parmesan cheese

1. Start by placing the tomatoes in your slow cooker, then add the stock, pesto, onion, garlic and Worcestershire sauce. Cook on low for 2–3 hours.

2. When the time is up, stir, then, using a hand blender, blitz the soup to a creamy consistency. If you feel at this point you need to add a little water to thin it out, please do so. It will all depend on how juicy and ripe your tomatoes are. Add the basil, season and cook for a further hour.

3. Meanwhile, make the croutons. Slice the baguette to make around 6 discs, drizzle with olive oil and evenly sprinkle the Parmesan over the top, along with a pinch of salt and pepper. Place in your air fryer and cook at 180°C for around 3–5 minutes until crisp. Alternatively, arrange the croutons on a baking sheet and cook in a preheated oven at 180°C/350°F/gas 4 for 8–10 minutes.

4. Serve your rich and creamy tomato soup with the croutons and enjoy.

Squash & Coconut Soup

COOK 5–6 hours on low   **SERVES** 4

I love making soups all year round, and this one in particular works well in any season. The combination of flavours is just incredible – the squash, coconut, chilli, turmeric and ginger pack a punch of flavour. And it's super healthy, too!

500g butternut squash, peeled
    and cut into cubes
1 tbsp olive oil
1 large onion, sliced
½ tsp chopped red chilli (if you
    don't like heat, leave it out)
1 tsp ground turmeric
1 x 400ml tin of coconut milk
1 carrot, grated
500ml vegetable stock
2 cloves of garlic, crushed
1 tsp curry powder
thumb-size piece of fresh ginger,
    peeled and grated
2 nuggets of frozen spinach
2 tbsp single cream (optional)
sea salt and freshly ground black
    pepper

To serve
single cream
a handful of steamed spinach

1. Put the butternut squash into your air fryer, drizzle with the olive oil and toss to coat. Cook at 180°C for 10 minutes, turning occasionally. Alternatively, arrange the squash in a roasting tray, toss with the oil and cook in the oven at 180°C/350°F/gas 4 for 15–20 minutes.

2. Transfer the squash to your slow cooker and add the rest of the ingredients except the spinach and cream. Cook on low for 4–5 hours, stirring occasionally. Add the spinach and cook for a further hour.

3. Using a hand blender, blitz the soup until smooth, then stir through the cream, if using. Season to taste.

4. Serve with a swirl of single cream and some steamed spinach leaves.

Pea & Mint Soup

COOK 1 hour 30 minutes on high   **SERVES** 6

This is the most refreshing soup. It also goes perfectly with any leftover gammon from my recipe on page 53. Simply dice some up and sprinkle on top when serving. Totally delicious.

1 bunch of spring onions,
   chopped
2 cloves of garlic, crushed
900g frozen peas
½ tsp caster sugar
900ml vegetable stock
a handful of fresh mint, chopped,
   plus a little extra to serve
½ tbsp lemon juice
sea salt and freshly ground black
   pepper

To serve
2 tbsp Greek yoghurt

1. Put the spring onions, garlic, peas and sugar into your slow cooker, pour in the stock, and cook on high for 1 hour 30 minutes.

2. Add the chopped mint and lemon juice, then blitz until smooth. If your soup is a little too thick for your liking, add a dash more water.

3. Season, then serve sprinkled with fresh mint and with a dollop of Greek yoghurt.

Red Cabbage

COOK 6 hours on low or 3 hours on high   **SERVES** 6 as a side dish

You can make this side dish ahead of time and freeze it – perfect for keeping the stress of Christmas dinner down!

2 tbsp olive oil

2 red onions, sliced

1 red cabbage, sliced

200ml vegetable stock

3 tbsp balsamic vinegar

100g brown sugar

1 large cooking apple, peeled and grated

¼ tsp grated nutmeg

sea salt and freshly ground black pepper

1. Preheat your slow cooker on low for 5 minutes.

2. Set the slow cooker to 'sauté'. Heat the olive oil in the slow cooker, add the onion and sauté for about 5–10 minutes, or do the same on the hob in a frying pan. Add the sliced cabbage and cook for a further 5 minutes. If you're using a separate pan add the onion and sliced cabbage into your slow cooker. Then add the rest of the ingredients and stir well. Cook on low for 6 hours or high for 3 hours.

Rosemary Roast Potatoes

COOK 3–4 hours on high   **SERVES** 4–6 as a side dish

I discovered the recipe for roasties in the slow cooker by complete accident. I planned to cook a chicken in the air fryer to have with some salad, but the chicken was too big to also cook the potatoes in the air fryer, so I decided to give the potatoes a go in the slow cooker instead. They did not disappoint! If you want them crispier, while your chicken is resting, give them a 5-minute blast in the air fryer at 180°C, or 10 minutes in a preheated oven at 180°C /350°F/gas 4.

8 medium potatoes, peeled and cut into chunks

2 tbsp olive oil

4 cloves of garlic, crushed and unpeeled

4 sprigs of fresh rosemary

sea salt and freshly ground black pepper

1. Put the potatoes into your slow cooker and drizzle with the olive oil. Season and add the garlic cloves. Place a tea towel over the top, close the lid and cook on high for 3–4 hours. I usually stir every hour or so, but it isn't necessary.

2. An hour before the end of the cooking time, add the rosemary.

3. Check to see if the potatoes are cooked through before serving, as they may need longer depending on their size.

New Potatoes with Capers & Lemon Butter

COOK 4 hours on high   **SERVES** 4 as a side dish

This recipe is such a vibrant dish that you can serve all year round. It's a great accompaniment to summer BBQs.

1kg new potatoes, halved (make sure they're all a similar size)

2 tbsp butter, melted

2 tbsp olive oil

juice of 1 lemon

2 tbsp capers

a few sprigs of fresh dill, chopped

sea salt and freshly ground black pepper

1. Put the new potatoes into your slow cooker and cook on high for 4 hours.

2. Just before the potatoes are ready, mix the butter with the olive oil and lemon juice, then stir in your capers along with about a tablespoon of the caper juice.

3. When the potatoes are cooked, pour over the butter mixture, toss well, season, then sprinkle over the fresh dill.

White Loaf

COOK 2 hours on high, and 30–40 minutes proving **SERVES** 4–6

It was my mum who suggested I try to cook a loaf of bread in the slow cooker. I was sceptical at first, but after my first attempt I couldn't believe the result. It was delicious. We served ours warm with some leftover tomato and basil soup we had made the day before. Scrumptious.

400g white bread flour, plus extra for dusting
5g fast-acting dried yeast
150ml whole milk
120ml warm water, plus a splash more if needed
1 tsp salt

1. In a large mixing bowl, mix the flour and yeast. Add the milk, water and salt, then mix well.

2. Dust some flour onto a clean surface, tip the dough out and begin to knead. I would knead for around 10 minutes. After 10 minutes your dough should become pliable and not too sticky; you would rather it a little too wet than too dry. Please do add a splash more water if your dough feels too dry at this stage.

3. Pop the dough back into your bowl and cover with a tea towel. Leave somewhere warm for around 30–40 minutes. After this time, knead again for about a minute or so, then form your dough into a neat, plump ball.

4. Line your slow cooker with baking paper and put in your dough. I like to place a tea towel over the top before closing the lid, as this captures the moisture. Cook on high for 2 hours.

5. Remove the lid and tea towel and leave for 20–30 minutes or so. Serve warm with one of my delicious soups and enjoy.

Crunchy Slaw

SERVES 4

Who doesn't love a slaw! I've found the cost of some readymade coleslaws to be rising, so I thought I'd make my own. We have ours in sandwiches, on jacket potatoes and it's also a great accompaniment to my Spicy Chicken Drumsticks (see page 90). Or as a side for The Ultimate Sloppy Joes (see page 70).

100g red cabbage, thinly sliced
1 carrot, grated
1 red onion, thinly sliced
100g Greek yoghurt
juice of 1 lemon
sea salt and freshly ground black
  pepper

1. Mix all the ingredients in a bowl until well combined, then season to taste.

Yoghurt & Mint Raita

SERVES 4

A wonderful side dip which goes perfectly with most curries. It's also great with the Tandoori Chicken Wraps (see page 93). And my Moroccan Lamb (see page 48).

200g plain yoghurt
¼ cucumber, finely chopped
a handful of fresh mint leaves,
  finely chopped
sea salt and freshly ground black
  pepper

1. Spoon the yoghurt into a bowl and season.

2. Drain the cucumber on kitchen paper, patting it dry to remove excess moisture, then add to the yoghurt. Add the mint and seasoning and mix until everything is well combined.

Rhubarb Chutney

COOK 6 hours on low   **MAKES** 2–3 jars
KIT muslin cloth or bag, sterilized jam jars (whatever sizes you have to hand)

Growing up, I was never a fan of chutney; I didn't quite get it. Now, I can't get enough of it! For me, it's a perfect accompaniment to any cheese sandwich and an absolute must for a tasty cheese board. Why not make extra and give the jars as little gifts to friends and family.

zest and juice of 2 lemons
thumb-sized piece of fresh ginger,
    peeled and chopped
1kg fresh rhubarb, finely chopped
4 large onions, finely chopped
300g sultanas
700g brown sugar
1 tsp salt
500ml cider vinegar
1 tsp cayenne pepper
1 tsp ground ginger

1. Place the lemon zest and ginger in a muslin cloth or bag, tying a knot at the end so the contents are secure, then set aside.

2. Put the rhubarb and onion into your slow cooker. Juice the lemons into the slow cooker, then add the sultanas, brown sugar, salt, vinegar and spices. Stir well.

3. Place your muslin into the slow cooker and cook on low for 6 hours. Remove the lid and leave to cool.

4. Spoon the chutney into your jam jars and make sure the mixture is thoroughly cool before you place on the lids.

5. Store in a cool, dry place. Once opened, store in the fridge for up to 5 weeks.

Mixed Berry Jam

COOK 2 hours on low   **MAKES** 2–3 jars
KIT sterilized jam jars (whatever sizes you have to hand)

Spoon into sterilized jam jars, then leave to cool before placing on the lids. It can be stored in the fridge for up to a month.

1kg mixed berries
1 tbsp honey
1 tbsp Chambord liqueur or
    brandy
400g preserving sugar

1. Place all the ingredients in your slow cooker, stir, then cook on low for 2 hours.

2. After 1 hour, remove the lid and keep an eye on your jam until you get the desired consistency, stirring now and then. Bear in mind the jam will set a little more as it cools.

3. Spoon into sterilized jars, then leave to cool before placing on the lids. It will keep in a cool, dry place for about a week.

Apple Sauce

COOK 4-5 hours on low   **MAKES** 2–3 jars

I love making apple sauce. It's an absolute must with a pork roast on a Sunday in our house. It's also delicious on porridge or with yoghurt for breakfast. This recipe freezes really well – I get such satisfaction knowing I have a batch in the freezer ready to go whenever I need it.

8 Bramley apples, peeled, cored and cut into cubes (about 2cm)
25g caster sugar
450ml water
juice of 1 lemon

1. Put the apples and sugar into your slow cooker, pour in the water and squeeze in the lemon juice. Cook on low for 4–5 hours.

2. If you would like to, you can use a potato masher or fork to make the apples a smoother consistency.

3. Allow to cool and keep in an airtight container in the fridge for up to 5 days, or freeze for up to 3 months.

Desserts & Drinks

Croissant & Butter Pudding

COOK 3 hours on low   **SERVES** 4

I love this twist on the classic – the croissants give it so much flavour. It feels like a real treat!

6 croissants
75g butter
100g marmalade
300ml whole milk
2 eggs
100g raisins
2 tbsp brown sugar

To serve
vanilla ice cream

1. Cut the croissants in half lengthways and spread each half with all the butter, then spread with the marmalade.

2. In a jug or bowl, beat together the milk and eggs.

3. Place half the croissants into the slow cooker, stacking them up against each other. Pour half the milk and egg mixture over the croissants and sprinkle over half of the raisins and sugar. Place the rest of the croissants on top to create a second layer, then pour over the rest of the milk and egg mixture and sprinkle over the rest of the raisins and sugar. Before putting the lid on the slow cooker, place a tea towel over it, then close the lid. This helps to soak up some of the moisture. Cook on low for 3 hours.

4. I like to release the lid and remove the tea towel about 15 minutes before I serve.

5. Perfect with a dollop of vanilla ice cream.

Boozy Pear & Apple Crumble

COOK 3 hours on high   **SERVES** 4

This recipe reminds me of Christmas. It's such a crowd-pleaser and makes your entire house smell scrumptious. By coating some of your fruit with cornflour before cooking, it creates a thicker, almost creamy, crumble filling.

110g cornflour

3 pears, peeled and thinly sliced

2 large cooking apples, peeled and thinly sliced

50ml dark rum

25ml ginger wine

1 tbsp ground ginger

2 cinnamon sticks

50ml water

1 tbsp runny honey

1 tbsp brown sugar

75g pistachios, crushed, plus extra to serve

For the crumble topping

75g porridge oats

125g plain flour

75g brown sugar

1 tsp ground cinnamon

125g butter, at room temperature

To serve

clotted cream or ice cream

1. Put your cornflour into a large bowl. Add half the sliced fruit and toss to coat.

2. Scatter all the fruit into the base of your slow cooker. Add the rum and ginger wine, ground ginger, cinnamon and water. Cook on high for 2 hours.

3. While your fruit is cooking, make your crumble topping. Put your porridge oats, flour, sugar, ground cinnamon and butter into a mixing bowl. Using your fingertips, rub all the ingredients together until all the ingredients are incorporated, then set aside.

4. After 2 hours of cooking time, stir your fruit well and add the honey and brown sugar. Remove the cinnamon sticks, then spoon the crumble topping over the fruit to cover it and scatter over the pistachios. Cook for a further hour.

5. Serve with clotted cream or ice cream and an extra sprinkling of crushed pistachios if you like a bit more crunch.

Sticky Toffee Pudding

COOK 8 hours on low **SERVES** 6

What can I say about sticky toffee pudding! It's an absolute classic and one that
I'd eat every single day if I could. I always serve mine with scrumptious vanilla ice cream.
Pure heaven . . .

125g butter
250g dates, stoned
125ml boiling water
1 tsp vanilla extract
275g brown sugar
325ml double cream
5 tbsp treacle
2 large eggs, beaten
200g self-raising flour
1 tsp bicarbonate of soda
sea salt

To serve
clotted cream, custard or
    ice cream

1. Preheat your slow cooker on low for 10 minutes and make sure your pudding bowl fits into your slow cooker when the lid is closed. Grease your bowl with tablespoon of the butter and line with baking paper.

2. Pop the dates into a heatproof bowl and cover with the boiling water. Leave to soak for 30 minutes.

3. Put the vanilla extract, 80g of the sugar, the cream, half the treacle and half the butter into a pan. Cook over a medium heat, stirring until the sugar dissolves. Carefully turn up the heat and cook for 3 more minutes. Whisk the mixture and add a pinch of salt. Pour about a third of the mixture into your lined bowl, leaving the rest to reheat later for your sauce.

4. Remove the dates from the bowl, reserving the water, and roughly chop. In a mixing bowl, stir together the remaining sugar, treacle and butter with the beaten eggs. Carefully fold in the flour, bicarbonate of soda, ¼ teaspoon of salt, the dates and soaking water. Spoon into the pudding bowl, leaving about a 1cm gap at the top. Cover with a greased layer of baking paper and a layer of tinfoil, then make a central cut to allow the steam to escape and tie with some string.

5. Place the bowl in your slow cooker. Boil the kettle and pour in the water to fill halfway up the bowl. Close the lid of the slow cooker and cook on low for 8 hours.

6. Carefully remove the pudding from your slow cooker. You may want to run a knife around the edge of the bowl before turning out onto a serving plate. When you are ready to serve, reheat the remaining sauce to pour over your pudding. Serve with clotted cream, custard or ice cream.

Desserts & Drinks

My Dad's Favourite Rice Pudding

COOK 3–4 hours on low   **SERVES** 4–6

This recipe does not compromise on flavour or comfort! It's my dad's absolute favourite pudding and is guaranteed to please.

2 tbsp butter
175g short grain pudding rice
400ml coconut milk
550–700ml milk
4 tbsp sugar
2 tbsp runny honey
140g clotted cream

To serve
Mixed Berry Jam (see page 164, optional)

1. Preheat your slow cooker on low for 10 minutes.

2. Grease the slow cooker with a tablespoon of the butter. Add the rice, coconut milk, 550ml of the milk, sugar and honey and dot in the remaining tablespoon of butter. Cook on low for 3–4 hours, stirring occasionally throughout.

3. Around 30 minutes before the end of the cooking time, add the clotted cream and stir. At this point you can add a little more milk if you prefer a thinner consistency.

4. Serve on its own or with a dollop of homemade jam.

Good Ol' Treacle Sponge Pudding

COOK 4 hours on high   **SERVES** 4–6

It wouldn't be a cookbook without putting one of the all-time greats in it, right! This is super delicious and proper comfort food. Top tip: if you want to make sure your pudding is cooked through before serving, insert a metal skewer or thin knife into the middle – it's done if it comes out clean.

185g butter, at room temperature

3 tbsp golden syrup

1 tbsp white breadcrumbs

180g caster sugar

zest of 1 orange

3 eggs, beaten

180g self-raising flour

2 tbsp whole milk

To serve

custard

1. First things first: make sure your pudding bowl fits into your slow cooker and you can close the lid properly. I would also preheat your slow cooker on low for 20 minutes for this recipe.

2. Grease the pudding bowl with about a tablespoon of butter. In a separate mixing bowl, mix the golden syrup and breadcrumbs, then tip this into the pudding bowl.

3. In the same mixing bowl, beat the remaining butter with the sugar and orange zest. Add the beaten eggs, but not all at once, just gradually. Carefully fold in the flour along with the milk, then spoon this mixture into your pudding bowl.

4. Cover the bowl with a buttered piece of tinfoil and make an opening in the centre to allow the pudding to rise. I like to tie the foil in place with some string too before I place the pudding bowl into the slow cooker. Cook on high for 4 hours.

5. Carefully remove the bowl from the slow cooker – it will be hot. Remove the foil and turn your pudding out on to a serving dish. Enjoy with some thick custard.

Festive Baked Apples

COOK 4–6 hours on low or 2 hours on high   **SERVES** 4

The smell of the spices mixed with the apples is just perfect – an ideal pudding to serve on an autumn day. You can also prepare this ahead of time and simply place the apples in your slow cooker when you're ready.

4 small Bramley apples

4 level tbsp mincemeat

1 tbsp runny honey

zest and juice of 1 large orange

½ tsp ground cinnamon

½ tsp ground ginger

To serve

vanilla ice cream or plain yoghurt

1. Carefully remove the core of each apple and set the apples aside.

2. In a mixing bowl, mix together the mincemeat, honey, orange zest and juice and spices until well combined. Spoon into the cored apples, then place them in your slow cooker. Cook on low for 4–6 hours or high for 2 hours.

3. When cooked, carefully transfer the apples to a serving dish, then pour over the juices in the bottom of the slow cooker.

4. Serve hot with some vanilla ice cream or plain yoghurt.

Naughty Milk Chocolate Fudge

COOK 1 hour on high, then 6 hours/overnight setting **SERVES** around 6

I'd never made fudge before, but last Easter I decided to try it out so I could give it as little gifts. This recipe is so delicious, I now can't stop making it! Add whatever toppings you like. We also like to use white chocolate buttons, Chocolate Orange, Flakes and After Eight mints. This recipe is also perfect to use up leftover chocolate from Christmas or Easter eggs – if you have any that is! It's a great one to get the kids involved in, too.

400g good-quality milk chocolate
1 x 397g tin of condensed milk
your favourite topping (I use crushed Crunchie bars)

1. Break the milk chocolate into chunks into your slow cooker. Add the condensed milk, then cook on high for 1 hour. I like to stir mine a few times throughout, but you don't have to; it just smells so good!

2. Meanwhile, line a deep baking tray with baking paper.

3. After the cooking time, pour the mixture into your lined baking tray and scatter over your chosen topping. Place the fudge in the fridge and leave to set for at least 6 hours (overnight is preferred).

4. Cut into bite-sized chunks and enjoy – it's perfect with a mid-morning cuppa!

Apple & Rum Punch

COOK 3 hours on low   **SERVES** 8–10

If you want to make an equally tasty but non-alcoholic version of this punch, just leave out the rum. To add a little flair to each cup, why not add some air dried apple slices, or make your own in the air fryer, both for decoration and an extra nibble . . .

2 litres apple juice
1 apple, thinly sliced
1 cinnamon stick
thumb-sized piece of fresh ginger, peeled
4 tbsp dark rum

1. Put all the ingredients except the rum into your slow cooker and cook on low for 3 hours.

2. Just before serving, add the rum and stir well before ladling into cups.

Mulled Wine

COOK at least 3 hours on low **SERVES** 12–14

The scrumptious aroma of this winter warmer filling the house is Christmas for me! This mulled wine is perfect if you're entertaining because it's so easy. Your guests will love it and I bet they will ask for the recipe. Whenever you're running low, simply add another bottle; just replace the lid for a while as it warms up.

3 bottles of red wine
3 shots of brandy
peel of 1 large orange, plus extra
    for serving
10 cloves
2 cinnamon sticks
2 tbsp maple syrup
a handful of fresh cranberries

1. Combine all the ingredients in your slow cooker and stir. Cook on low for at least 3 hours, or as long as you need (keep the lid closed until you're ready to serve).

2. Serve in heatproof glasses, with a slice of orange peel on the rim.

Index

Index

Thank You

I am so fortunate to have such a wonderful support network in my life. I don't and won't ever take any of you for granted. I wouldn't be where I am today without the unfailing love and support of my wonderful parents. My amazing son Jack, who has been by my side and supported me every step of this incredible journey, I love you. My sister, always at the end of the phone, no matter how near or far apart we are. And my aunty Net, for always being so positive and full of advice. To my partner Will, the most encouraging, patient and supportive partner I could ever wish for. I am thankful every day that I have you in my life. You are all truly my world, so thank you from the bottom of my heart.

To the outstanding team at Penguin Michael Joseph, you all work so incredibly hard, and I really feel grateful every day that we are part of the same 'Ultimate Cookbook' Team. The amazingly talented Dan Hurst, Aggie Russell, Sophie Elletson, Georgie Hewitt, Danielle Wood, Ted Allen, Katy McClelland, Troy Willis, Arnaud Berrabia, Sarah Birks, Ellie Morley and Kallie Townsend. Your encouragement and never-ending support have been without a doubt life changing. A special thanks to Dan Hurst: without you, none of this would be happening, thank you for believing in me.

Hungry for more delicious meals from the money and time saving expert, Clare Andrews? Pick up your copy of the *Sunday Times* bestselling *The Ultimate Air Fryer Cookbook* now . . .

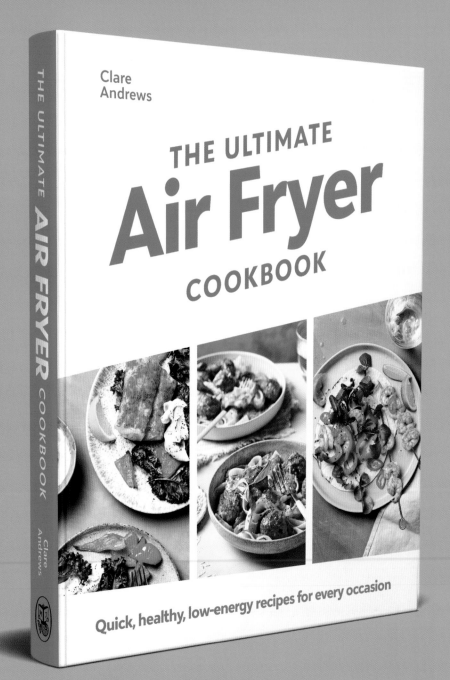